P9-DHT-001

QUIET MOMENTS
for a WOMAN'S HEART

QUIET MOMENTS
for a WOMAN'S HEART

encouragement to warm
your heart and
lift your spirit

BETHANYHOUSE
MINNEAPOLIS, MINNESOTA

Quiet Moments™ for a Woman's Heart

Copyright © 2008 by GRQ Inc.

Scripture quotations noted AMP are from The Amplified Bible, Old Testament. Copyright © 1965, 1987 by The Zondervan Corporation. The Amplified New Testament, copyright © 1954, 1958, 1987 by The Lockman Foundation. Used by permission.

Scripture quotations noted CEV are taken from The Contemporary English Version. Copyright © 1995 by the American Bible Society. Used by permission.

Scripture quotations noted ESV are from The Holy Bible, English Standard Version, copyright © 2001 by Crossway Bibles, a division of Good News Publishers. Used by permission. All rights reserved.

Scripture quotations noted GNT are from the Good News Translation, Second Edition, copyright © 1992 by American Bible Society. Used by permission. All rights reserved.

Scripture quotations noted HCSB have been taken from the Holman Christian Standard Bible®, Copyright © 1999, 2000, 2002, 2003 by Holman Bible Publishers. Used by permission. Holman Christian Standard Bible®, Holman CSB® and HCSB® are federally registered trademarks of Holman Bible Publishers.

Scripture quotations noted MSG are taken from *The Message* by Eugene H. Peterson. Copyright © 1993, 1994, 1995, 1996, 2000, 2001, 2002. Used by permission of NavPress Publishing Group. All rights reserved.

Scripture quotations noted NASB are taken from the New American Standard Bible® Copyright © 1960, 1962, 1963–1968, 1971, 1973–1975, 1977, 1995 by the Lockman Foundation. Used by permission.

Scripture quotations noted NCV are from The Holy Bible, New Century Version, copyright © 1987, 1988, 1991 by Word Publishing, a division of Thomas Nelson, Inc. All rights reserved. Used by permission.

Scripture quotations noted NIV are taken from the Holy Bible: New International Version (North American Edition)®. Copyright © 1973–1978, 1984, by the International Bible Society. Used by permission of Zondervan. All rights reserved.

Scripture quotations noted NKJV are taken from The New King James Version. Copyright © 1979, 1980, 1982, Thomas Nelson, Inc., Publishers.

Scripture quotation noted NLT are taken from the *Holy Bible*, New Living Translation, copyright © 1996, 2004. Used by permission of Tyndale House Publishers, Inc., Wheaton, Illinois 60189. All rights reserved.

All rights reserved. No part of this publication may be reproduced, stored in a retrieval system, or transmitted in any form or by any means—electronic, mechanical, photocopying, recording, or any other—without the prior written permission of the publisher. The only exception is brief quotations in printed reviews.

Published by Bethany House Publishers
11400 Hampshire Avenue South
Bloomington, Minnesota 55438

Bethany House Publishers is a division of Baker Publishing Group, Grand Rapids, Michigan.

ISBN 10: 0-7642-0453-X
ISBN 13: 978-0-7642-0453-1

Editor: Teri Wilhelms
Associate Editor: Natasha Sperling
Project Manager: Michael R. Briggs
Manuscript written and prepared by Jan Coleman & the Snapdragon Group
Design: Diane Whisner

Printed in the United States of America.

08 09 10—5 4 3 2 1

I'm asking GOD for one thing, only one thing:
To live with him in his house my whole life long. . . .
That's the only quiet, secure place in a noisy world,
The perfect getaway, far from the buzz of traffic.

Psalm 27:4–5 MSG

CONTENTS

Introduction 8

1. Quiet Corners 10
2. He Is There 13
3. The Pause to Refresh 16
4. Like One of These 19
5. Reach Out and Touch 22
6. Just As It Is 25
7. Mirroring the Good 28
8. What If? 31
9. Character Review 34
10. Unexpected Joy 37
11. Focusing on God 40
12. Turning Pages 43
13. A Jar of Gratitude 46
14. Especially for You 49
15. Trivial Pursuits 52
16. A Heartfelt Thank-You 55
17. Unsinkable Optimism 58
18. Basking in Bubbles 61
19. You Deserve It 64
20. Keep It Simple 67
21. Stairway to Heaven 70
22. Praise God 73
23. Express Yourself 76
24. *Selah* 79
25. Tomorrow Is Another Day 82
26. Deepest Desires 85
27. Keeping Watch 88
28. Nourishing Moments 91
29. If You Want the Rainbow 94
30. Family Focus 97

31. Soothing With Song.. 100

32. Celebrate! 103

33. In a Child's Eyes... 106

34. Power Checkup 109

35. A Friend Indeed.. 112

36. The Not-So-Impossible Dream 115

37. Rest Stops 118

38. Spirit Shape-Up 121

39. Daily Laughter 124

40. Words of Love 127

41. Precious Treasure 130

42. The Best of Friends 133

43. The Gift of Today 136

44. Deep Roots... 139

45. Inner Light 142

46. Soothe Yourself 145

47. Enjoy the Ordinary.. 148

48. Remembering Why.. 151

49. It's a Wonderful Life 154

50. Free As a Bird 157

51. Breathing Deep 160

52. Get Away 163

53. God's Plan.. 166

54. Gold Medal Performance 169

55. Aiming for Excellence... 172

56. Time to Let It Go 175

57. Take a Chance.. 178

58. Daily Joy 181

59. Love Comes Back...184

60. Quiet Within... 187

INTRODUCTION

We need quiet time to examine our lives openly and honestly. . . . Spending quiet time alone gives your mind an opportunity to renew itself and create order.

Susan Taylor

If you're like most women, you have very little "me" time. You are constantly moving throughout the day trying to complete all the tasks you've set out for yourself. There are so many things to do and people to care for; it's often not possible to find time for yourself. Wouldn't it be nice to slip away for some personal comfort time?

Quiet Moments for a Woman's Heart presents a gentle invitation to slow down and unwind. You'll discover soothing insights that refresh your mind with an inspiring word and offer a peaceful place where your spirit can be renewed.

Presented here are selected inspirational writings, quotes, Bible verses, poems, and meditations—the format invites reading for thirty seconds or an hour. You can open the book to any page and find something heartwarming, something that strikes home. *Quiet Moments for a Woman's Heart* will become a personal and valued tool for replenishing your inner resources.

The opening lines of Max Ehrmann's famous poem "Desiderata" begin: "Go placidly amid the noise and haste, and remember what peace there may be in silence." One of the best things you can do for yourself is to save some time for a little silence in your day.

Find a quiet place and settle in to your own personal moment. You will discover encouragement, strength, insight, and food for thought. *Quiet Moments for a Woman's Heart* is filled with inspiration about God's involvement in the details of our lives, how to listen for God's voice, encouragement to have faith and trust in his influence on life events, and how with God all things are possible.

> *When was the last time you spent a quiet moment just doing nothing—just sitting and looking at the sea, or watching the wind blowing the tree limbs, or waves rippling on a pond, a flickering candle or children playing in the park?*
>
> Ralph Marston

QUIET CORNERS

A Moment to Rest

Do you long for a quiet corner? A place to get away from the overload of daily life—rush-hour traffic, insistent telephones, unending e-mail messages? You are not alone. Some women have discovered monasteries where guests can gain distance from the world, eat simple meals in silence, stroll on winding trails, contemplate, and pray. One visitor described it as a "detox center" for her spirit.

> *Practice the art of aloneness and you will discover the treasure of tranquility. Develop the art of solitude and you will unearth the gift of serenity.*
>
> William Arthur Ward

A monastery retreat isn't always possible, but you can create your own private haven at home or close by, an oasis where you can spend some downtime. Find a good spot to unwind—a comfortable chair in a quiet room, a shady garden, your porch or patio, a nearby park, greenway, or beach—enjoy some tea, coffee, or juice, and relax your mind and body after the rigors of the day.

Pause for a deep breath, refresh your mind with inspiring words, and focus on yourself and how God can help fulfill your needs. As you dwell in the beauty of the heavenly perspective, you'll be reminded of all God has in store for you right now.

Solitude can be your best companion. In the stillness of your heart, you can regenerate and renew.

A Moment to Reflect

The result of righteousness will be peace; the effect of
righteousness will be quiet confidence forever.
Then my people will dwell in a peaceful place,
and in safe and restful dwellings.

Isaiah 32:17–18 HCSB

Nothing soothes your inner being more than being alone in a quiet place. Make an appointment with yourself for quiet time in your own little corner of the world. God will meet you in your sanctuary. Just name the time and place. Prepare yourself by leaving behind agendas, schedules, and to-do lists. Deliberately let go of your cares and relax your body and mind. Let God's presence surround you as you discover more about yourself and the One who loves you. Allow God to restore you to wholeness. He will give you a new perspective, refresh your mind, and give you the fuel to move through whatever tomorrow may bring.

There is time in which to be, simply to be,
that time in which God quietly tells us who we are
and who he wants us to be.
It is then that God can take our emptiness
and fill it up with what he wants,
and drain away the business
with which we inevitably get involved
in the dailyness of human living.

Madeleine L'Engle

A Moment to Refresh

Loneliness is inner emptiness. Solitude is inner fulfillment. Solitude is a state of mind and heart.

Richard Foster

❦

If you have an important decision to make or you find yourself in circumstances where you do not know what is best to do or answer, spend at least one night in meditation. You will not be sorry.

Amish Proverb

How priceless is your unfailing love! Both high and low among men find refuge in the shadow of your wings.

Psalm 36:7 NIV

❦

I have calmed and quieted my soul, like a weaned child with its mother; like a weaned child is my soul within me.

Psalm 131:2 ESV

He makes me to lie down in green pastures; He leads me beside the still waters. He restores my soul.

Psalm 23:2–3 NKJV

❦

You, the LORD's people, will live in peace, calm and secure.

Isaiah 32:18 CEV

❦

O God, You are awesome from Your sanctuary. The God of Israel Himself gives strength and power to the people. Blessed be God!

Psalm 68:35 NASB

HE IS THERE

God is with you now. He is as near as your heartbeat, as close as your breath. Focus on God's presence. Be aware that he is there with you. Curl up in a large, comfy chair. Picture yourself as a child, snuggling with your perfect Father—one who will love you, protect you, cherish you, hold you close, and give you his strength, throughout eternity.

Relax in the comfort of his arms, almighty yet tender. Picture yourself leaning against his powerful presence, moving ever so gently with the force of his own life-giving breath. Delight in his love for you. Take pleasure in his joy over the one-of-a-kind design he used to create you.

> *Wait upon God and feel his good presence; this will carry you evenly through your day's business.*
>
> William Penn

Speak to him—aloud, if you feel comfortable. Tell him how much it means to know he's near. Tell him how safe you feel, how grateful you are for his love. Whisper your secrets, even the ones you've never spoken aloud. Thank him for the difference his presence has made in your life.

Finish by sitting quietly. Listen for God's voice, speaking to you alone. Acknowledge his loving presence, knowing that it is eternal, knowing that he is always there.

A Moment to Reflect

*Rejoice in the Lord always; again I will say, Rejoice. Let
your reasonableness be known to everyone.
The Lord is at hand; do not be anxious about
anything, but in everything by prayer and
supplication with thanksgiving let your
requests be made known to God.*

Philippians 4:4–6 ESV

In the Old Testament, God's presence often came in a visible form, such as a cloud or a burning bush. After Moses spent time with God, those who saw him could tell something extraordinary had happened—his face glowed from getting just a glimpse of God.

Though God's presence seemed more dramatic—and tangible—in the Old Testament, it was less accessible. With God's gift of the Holy Spirit given at Pentecost, people were then able to consistently experience God's presence in their lives. As God's beloved daughter, celebrate that privilege and remind yourself daily that God is near.

*Let the sweet hope that thou art mine my path of life attend; Thy
presence thro' my journey shine, and crown my journey's end.*

Anne Steele

❧

*The LORD is near to all who call on him, to all who call on
him in truth. He fulfills the desire of all who fear him;
he also hears their cry, and saves them. The LORD
watches over all who love him.*

Psalm 145:18–20 NRSV

May [the Lord] strengthen your hearts so that you will be blameless and holy in the presence of our God and Father when our Lord Jesus comes with all his holy ones.

1 Thessalonians 3:13 NIV

❧

As a mother comforts her child, so I'll comfort you.

Isaiah 66:13 MSG

❧

I am always with You.

Psalm 73:23 HCSB

❧

I have learned to feel safe and satisfied, just like a young child on its mother's lap.

Psalm 131:2 CEV

❧

You have made known to me the ways of life; you will make me full of gladness with your presence.

Acts 2:28 NRSV

❧

Draw near to God and He will draw near to you.

James 4:8 NASB

God is always near you and with you; leave Him not alone.

Brother Lawrence

❧

God is not far away from us. Rather he awaits us every instant in our action, in the work of the moment. There is a sense in which he is at the tip of my pen, my spade, my brush, my needle.

Pierre Teilhard de Chardin

THE PAUSE TO REFRESH

A Moment to Rest

Do you sometimes feel like you can't get enough sleep? You're going full tilt and can't get the rest you need? If only you could grab a little nap. Don't feel guilty; resting is not selfish. Renewal isn't a convenience reserved for a lady of leisure, it's a "must do" if you want to stay stable and sane in today's world. Reward yourself with slumber whenever you get the chance. It's one of the best things you can do for both mind and body.

I will lie down and sleep in peace, for you alone, O LORD, make me dwell in safety.

Psalm 4:8 NIV

The best time for a nap is when you're on the run and seemingly have no time. Don't wait for exhaustion to overtake you—find a quiet spot for a twenty- or thirty-minute nap. Fold your hands over your chest, close your eyes, breathe deeply, and drift off. Set worries and concerns aside for a few minutes.

Sleep soothes, restores, and regenerates. Remember Sleeping Beauty? After pricking her finger on the spinning wheel, she fell into a long, deep sleep, but after a prince's kiss she woke up more beautiful than ever, to a life of promise and hope. Sleep is where God will touch the depths of your heart and mind with his caring hand.

A Moment to Reflect

*Jesus said, "Let's go to a place where we
can be alone and get some rest."*

Mark 6:31 CEV

An amazing thing happens when the body is resting. The body purifies itself by removing toxins, restoring cells, and relaxing muscles. As a field that is rested for a season gives more abundant crops, so a woman who is rested can give of herself more fully and is more gratified in the giving.

Many Scriptures in the Bible refer to sleep and rest. Even God rested from his work on the seventh day to show us how important it is. So enjoy a short siesta. As you sleep, God will soothe your weariness. His wisdom will filter gently through your quiet mind. When you wake, you'll have more energy to be your best.

*Sleep is the celestial nurse who croons away our consciousness, and God deals with the unconscious life of the soul in places where only he and his angels have charge.
As you retire to rest, give your soul and God a time together, and commit your life to God with a
conscious peace for the hours of sleep.*

Oswald Chambers

*The LORD preserves the simple;
I was brought low, and He saved me.
Return to your rest, O my soul,
For the LORD has dealt bountifully with you.*

Psalm 116:6–7 NASB

A Moment to Refresh

"Holy leisure" refers to a sense of balance in life, an ability to be at peace throughout the activities of the day, an ability to rest and take time to enjoy beauty, an ability to pace ourselves.

Richard Foster

❧

O bed! O bed! delicious bed! That heaven upon earth to the weary head.

Thomas Hood

Come to me, all who labor and are heavy laden, and I will give you rest. Take my yoke upon you, and learn from me, for I am gentle and lowly in heart, and you will find rest for your souls. For my yoke is easy, and my burden is light.

Matthew 11:28–30 ESV

❧

I lie down and sleep;
I wake again, because the LORD sustains me.

Psalm 3:5 NIV

❧

On the seventh day God ended His work which He had done, and He rested on the seventh day from all His work which He had done. Then God blessed the seventh day and sanctified it, because in it He rested from all His work which God had created and made.

Genesis 2:2–3 NKJV

❧

The promise of "arrival" and "rest" is still there for God's people.
God himself is at rest. And at the end of the journey we'll surely rest with God.

Hebrews 4:9–10 MSG

LIKE ONE OF THESE

A Moment to Rest

Find a flower. It could be an iris from an arrangement on your kitchen table, a rose in your garden, a lily in the field, or even a pesky dandelion in your driveway. Hold the flower in your hand. Feel the velvety petals, the strong stem, and the texture of its leaves.

Smell it. Is there a fragrance? Study it. Explore every detail that makes it beautiful, every curve and line, the color of the blossom and shades of green on the stem and leaves. Is there anything that is considered common? If so, what and why?

> *Flowers are the sweetest things that God ever made, and forgot to put a soul into.*
>
> Henry Ward Beecher

Consider the hand that fashioned it is the same hand that fashioned you. Take a look in the mirror. Explore every detail, every curve and line of your own face. How has God made it beautiful? How is it different from those around you? Is there anything that you consider common? If so, what and why?

Take a moment with God. Speak to him and tell him, from your heart, how you feel about the face that he created for you. Then sit quietly and listen for God's response. He longs for you to fully know and enjoy what a beautiful woman you are.

A Moment to Reflect

*As for man, his days are as grass; as a flower of the field,
so he flourishes. For the wind passes over it and it is
gone. . . . But the mercy and loving-kindness of the Lord
are from everlasting to everlasting upon those who
reverently and worshipfully fear Him.*

Psalm 103:15–17 AMP

Movies, TV, magazines, and Web sites often push a narrow view of beauty. God's creations reflect his glory and have nothing to do with hair color or a wrinkle-free complexion. The beauty God created defies comparison. What is more beautiful, a cheetah or a sunset? An orchid or an ocean shore?

Learning to appreciate God's workmanship and image as reflected in yourself, others, and the world around you can soothe your spirit and foster contentment and praise. Viewing yourself as a one-of-a-kind, priceless work of art—and heart—will help you see yourself through God's eyes. It's a beautiful view.

*Turn my soul into a garden, where the flowers dance in the
gentle breeze, praising You with their beauty. Let my soul
be filled with beautiful virtues; let me be inspired by
Your Holy Spirit; let me praise You always.*

Teresa of Avila

*He covers the heavens with clouds; he prepares rain for the
earth; he makes grass grow on the hills.*

Psalm 147:8 ESV

Consider the lilies, how they grow: they neither toil nor spin; and yet I say to you, even Solomon in all his glory was not arrayed like one of these.

Luke 12:27 NKJV

❧

See! The winter is past; the rains are over and gone. Flowers appear on the earth; the season of singing has come.

Song of Solomon 2:11–12 NIV

❧

The wilderness and the dry land will be glad; the desert will rejoice and blossom like a rose.

Isaiah 35:1 HCSB

❧

Ever since the world was created, people have seen the earth and sky. Through everything God made, they can clearly see his invisible qualities—his eternal power and divine nature. So they have no excuse for not knowing God.

Romans 1:20 NLT

❧

Flowers and grass fade away, but what our God has said will never change.

Isaiah 40:8 CEV

'Tis my faith that every flower enjoys the air it breathes.

William Wordsworth

❧

Many flowers open to the sun, but only one follows him constantly—Heart, be thou the sunflower, not only open to receive God's blessing, but constant in looking to him.

Jean Paul Richter

REACH OUT AND TOUCH

A Moment to Rest

As you set aside regular times to rest, strengthen, and give to yourself, use them to become more aware of the needs of others outside your world. Feeling good inside can inspire you to reach out and share.

> *A cheerful heart does not count the cost of what he gives. His heart is set on pleasing and cheering him to whom the gift is given.*
>
> Julian of
> Norwich

Put yourself empathically in another's shoes as you read the daily paper, watch the news, or check the Internet for the latest headlines. See and hear the stories not as news but as individuals loved by God.

Can you picture yourself as the mother trying to care for her family in a famine, the stockholder who lost her life's savings through corrupt management, or a wife whose husband has died in a military training exercise? Visualize what you would need from others and what you would long for from God.

While it's not your job to solve the world's problems, you can make a difference in the lives of some. Pray for all those you've read about. Prayer is one way of touching lives that are far removed from your own. And that's all God asks from you—that you reach out to help those in need and to make the world a better place.

A Moment to Reflect

Share with God's people who are in need. Practice
hospitality. . . . Live in harmony with one another.
Do not be proud. . . . If it is possible, as far as it
depends on you, live at peace with everyone. . . . "If your
enemy is hungry, feed him; if he is thirsty, give him
something to drink." . . . Overcome evil with good.

Romans 12:13, 16, 18, 20–21 NIV

You are the face of an invisible God. While God has the power to miraculously heal a broken heart or to supply a basic need, he usually uses people, just like you, to make his love visible to a hurting world. He will teach you to share his love.

As you become more sensitive to the needs that surround you, you become more aware of the material, physical, and spiritual gifts God has given you. God will work through you to help others. You may become the answer to someone else's prayer. Reach out and touch someone's life.

Have you had a kindness shown? Pass it on;
'Twas not given for thee alone, Pass it on;
Let it travel down the years,
Let it wipe another's tears,
'Til in Heaven the deed appears—Pass it on.

Henry Burton

❧

Do all you can for everyone who deserves your help.

Proverbs 3:27 CEV

A Moment to Refresh

A kind heart is a fountain of gladness, making everything in its vicinity freshen into smiles.

Washington Irving

❧

You will find, as you look back upon your life, that the moments that stand out are the moments when you have done things for others.

Henry Drummond

Whoever is kind to the poor lends to the LORD, and will be repaid in full.

Proverbs 19:17 NRSV

❧

Do you have the gift of helping others? Do it with all the strength and energy that God supplies. Then everything you do will bring glory to God through Jesus Christ.

1 Peter 4:11 NLT

❧

Rejoice with those who rejoice, and weep with those who weep.

Romans 12:15 NASB

❧

His divine power has given us everything we need for life and godliness through our knowledge of him who called us by his own glory and goodness.

2 Peter 1:3 NIV

❧

Whoever despises his neighbor is a sinner, but blessed is he who is generous to the poor.

Proverbs 14:21 ESV

JUST AS IT IS

A Moment to Rest

When Moses and the Israelites were trapped at the Red Sea, God brought them miraculously through. Yet two months later, the Israelites were weary and tired of eating the same old food. They complained, "Why can't we be back in Egypt?" Did they truly want captivity again? No. They had simply forgotten God's faithfulness and felt pressured. In their frustration, they missed the lesson: Contentment is not the fulfillment of what one has; it is the realization of how much one already has.

Many people view happiness as a future state, something to achieve later, when a certain goal is reached. Have you ever reached that goal only to find the happiness short-lived? Once you got what you thought you wanted, were you happy with it? Have you ever reached a goal only to find yourself already looking for something else to give you a sense of fulfillment?

> *The children of Israel did not find in the manna all the sweetness and strength they might have found in it; not because the manna didn't contain them, but because they longed for other meat.*
>
> St. John of the Cross

Think about all the things you love about your life. Jot down a list of everything you already have. Ignore what might be or how you wish things could be in an ideal world. Contentment is sweet. Cultivate an appreciation for life just as it is.

A Moment to Reflect

Showing respect to the LORD brings true life — if you do it,
you can relax without fear of danger.

Proverbs 19:23 CEV

Paul's letter reminded the Philippians they should be
content with what they had. He urged them to try to
understand the difference between what they may have
wanted and what they actually needed. That is God's
desire for you as well.

God will supply every need, whether physical or emo-
tional, whether nourishment for the body, the mind,
or spirit. By trusting in God completely, your attitudes
and desires become his. Your priorities will change.
Trust him with your needs, to make you content, and
to keep you safe. You will feel full and satisfied with
what he provides, no matter what happens.

O what a happy soul am I! Although I cannot see,
I am resolved that in this world
Contented I will be; how many blessings I enjoy
That other people don't!
To weep and sigh because I'm blind, I cannot, and I won't.

Fanny J. Crosby

Not that I speak in regard to need, for I have learned in
whatever state I am, to be content. . . . Everywhere and in all
things I have learned both to be full and to be hungry,
both to abound and to suffer need. I can do all
things through Christ who strengthens me.

Philippians 4:11–13 NKJV

*Blessed is the one who finds wisdom, and
the one who gets understanding.*

Proverbs 3:13 ESV

❧

*Godliness with contentment is great gain.
For we brought nothing into this world,
and it is certain we can carry nothing out.
And having food and clothing, with
these we shall be content.*

1 Timothy 6:6–8 NKJV

❧

*Keep your lives free from the love of money and
be content with what you have, because God
has said, "Never will I leave you; never
will I forsake you." So we say
with confidence, "The Lord is my
helper; I will not be afraid.
What can man do to me?"*
Hebrews 13:5–6 NIV

❧

*On a good day enjoy yourself;
On a bad day examine your conscience.
God arranges for both kinds of days
So that we won't take anything for granted.*
Ecclesiastes 7:14 MSG

*When life isn't the
way you like, like
it the way it is.*

Jewish Proverb

❧

*Sweet are the
thoughts that
savor content;
The quiet mind
is richer than
a crown.*

Robert Greene

MIRRORING THE GOOD

A Moment to Rest

Pause for a moment and think about the women who have consistently been an encouragement to you, through either their words, their actions, or their example. One might be a family member or close friend who has been there for you during difficult times, or someone you worked with who urged you forward in your career. It might be someone who encouraged you in your relationship with God.

Encouragement is oxygen to the soul.

George M. Adams

As each person comes to mind, pause and picture her standing before you. Reflect on the specific ways she has encouraged you. Did her quirky sense of humor cheer you? Did her wise advice enable you to solve a dilemma or make a difficult decision? Did you want to become the type of woman she modeled for you? Thank God for that person.

After you've spent some time remembering these wonderful women, return the favor and refresh their spirits. Write a brief note to each woman, thanking her for the way she encouraged you. Tell each one how you see God's image brightly mirrored in her life, and mention what you have learned about the gift of encouragement from her godly example. In the process, you will undoubtedly encourage her in return.

A Moment to Reflect

*You see your face in a mirror and your
thoughts in the minds of others.*

Proverbs 27:19 CEV

Every characteristic you appreciate in the people who
mean the most to you is a reflection of God's character
in them. It's a glimpse of God that draws you near to
him when you feel that spark of love, friendship, and
encouragement in others.

When people in your life do something that encourages
you, don't just make a point of thanking them. Be sure
to also thank God for the beauty of his own perfect
character that you see has been mirrored in their lives.
Meditate on the characteristic that most deeply touches
your heart at the moment. Then ask him for wisdom
and strength to more fully develop that characteristic in
your own life so you, too, can mirror the good.

*Make it a rule, and pray to God to help you keep it, never, if
possible, to lie down at night without being able to say: "I
have made one human being at least a little wiser, or a little
happier, or at least a little better this day."*

Charles Kingsley

❧

*One man gives freely, yet gains even more; another withholds
unduly, but comes to poverty. A generous man will prosper;
he who refreshes others will himself be refreshed.*

Proverbs 11:24–25 NIV

A Moment to Refresh

Let us consider how to stimulate one another to love and good deeds, not forsaking our own assembling together, as is the habit of some, but encouraging one another.

Hebrews 10:24–25 NASB

❦

[Paul said,] "Encourage each other and build each other up, just as you are already doing."

1 Thessalonians 5:11 NLT

❦

God our Father loves us. He is kind and has given us eternal comfort and a wonderful hope. We pray that our Lord Jesus Christ and God our Father will encourage you and help you always to do and say the right thing.

2 Thessalonians 2:16–17 CEV

❦

Jonathan, Saul's son, visited David at Horesh and encouraged him in God.

1 Samuel 23:16 MSG

❦

Encourage each other daily, while it is still called today, so that none of you is hardened by sin's deception.

Hebrews 3:13 HCSB

Praise, like gold and diamonds, owes its value only to its scarcity.

Samuel Johnson

❦

Encouragement costs you nothing to give, but it is priceless to receive.

Author Unknown

WHAT IF?

A Moment to Rest

Worry can be a big problem. It's not uncommon to worry or to take cares to bed and then wake up with a weight on one's mind. Because women are designed to nurture and protect others, it's hard to see loved ones struggle. Some women think, *What if . . . ?*

Post this on your refrigerator:

KNEAD TODAY'S BREAD ONLY—TODAY'S BREAD IS THE ONLY BREAD I CAN POSSIBLY EAT.

And pray: Dear God, I know the things I worry about usually never happen. Help me focus on today. Tomorrow will take care of itself.

When you find yourself loaded down with negative possibilities, crowd them out. Grab those worrisome thoughts, secure them with a big knot, and give them to God. Write your worries in the sand on the beach and watch the tide sweep them away. Mentally stuff them into a burlap sack and watch them round the bend in the river—they'll not return, because they can't float back upstream on their own.

> *If only we could stop lamenting and look up. God is here. Christ is risen. The Spirit has been poured out from on high. All this we know as theological truth. It remains for us to turn it into joyous spiritual experience.*
>
> A. W. Tozer

What if? What if you let go and let God take care of you? What if you leave everything in God's hands? God will not let you down. He is always with you.

A Moment to Reflect

*Cast your cares on the LORD and he will
sustain you; he will never let the righteous fall.*

Psalm 55:22 NIV

There is a difference between planning and worrying.
One is time well spent, the other is time wasted. Worry
never changes a thing except the worrier.

When you crowd out worry, you send anxiety packing.
It's only when tomorrow's cares are added to today's
that the weight is more than you can bear. God never
intended you to worry, to fret over things beyond your
control. When you concentrate on God's promises to
meet all your needs, you fend off tensions of this
world. God will replace your cares with strength to
endure what happens both today and tomorrow.

*In prayerful moments subtle peace comes when I choose to
drop my fearful baggage into Greater Arms.*

Charlotte Adelsperger

*Jesus said, "Can any of you by worrying add a single hour
to your span of life? If then you are not able to do so small a
thing as that, why do you worry about the rest? Consider the
lilies, how they grow: they neither toil nor spin. . . . If God so
clothes the grass of the field, which is alive today and
tomorrow is thrown into the oven, how much more
will he clothe you—you of little faith!"*

Luke 12:25–28 NRSV

Jesus said, "Peace I leave with you, My peace I give to you; not as the world gives do I give to you. Let not your heart be troubled, neither let it be afraid."

John 14:27 NKJV

❧

Jesus said, "In me you may have peace. In the world you will have tribulation. But take heart; I have overcome the world."

John 16:33 ESV

❧

Jesus said, "Do not worry about your life, what you will eat or drink; or about your body, what you will wear. Is not life more important than food, and the body more important than clothes? Look at the birds of the air; they do not sow or reap or store away in barns, and yet your heavenly Father feeds them. . . . Do not worry about tomorrow, for tomorrow will worry about itself."

Matthew 6:25–26, 34 NIV

❧

Don't worry in advance about how to answer the charges against you, for I will give you the right words.

Luke 21:14–15 NLT

Worry gives a small thing a big shadow.

Swedish Proverb

❧

When worry is present, trust cannot crowd its way in.

Billy Graham

CHARACTER REVIEW

A Moment to Rest

Life is the classroom for character. It's time to review what you've learned. Review what the last twelve months have brought your way. Think of the relationships that have entered your life. Reflect on the victories, as well as the challenges, you've faced. Write down what you've discovered about yourself, about God, and about those you've been around in the past year. In what ways have you become a better woman?

When you've finished writing, reread what you've written. Take time to thank God for the confident person he's helping you become. Praise him for his lessons. Ask him for help in areas where you could use a little extra tutoring.

Anyone who keeps learning stays young.

Henry Ford

When you're finished, write "character review" on next year's calendar, one year from today's date. Finish by putting today's paper in a safe place, where you can review it next year. It will serve as a reminder of how far you've come.

Teachers know the importance of reviewing and testing students on what they've learned. They know this process helps plant information and skills more firmly in students' minds. As a student of life, reviewing what you've learned will keep your character fresh, leading you toward growth and maturity.

A Moment to Reflect

If the axe is dull and he does not sharpen its edge,
then he must exert more strength. Wisdom
has the advantage of giving success.

Ecclesiastes 10:10 NASB

Spiritual learning has many benefits and rewards. A person who grows by learning something new is vibrantly alive. A person who approaches life with wonder, a thirst for knowledge, and a desire to grow can be described as eager—eager to grow in faith, eager to approach life, eager to learn, and eager to mature.

When God reveals something in your life that you need to change, embrace it with enthusiasm. Make a point to learn from it and grow. Becoming the woman God created you to be is a day-by-day, year-by-year process of which learning is an integral part.

Take your needle, my child, and work at your pattern; it will
come out a rose by and by. Life is like that; one stitch
at a time taken patiently, and the pattern will
come out all right, like embroidery.

Oliver Wendell Holmes

Whatever is noble, whatever is right, whatever is pure, what-
ever is lovely, whatever is admirable—if anything is excellent
or praiseworthy—think about such things. Whatever you
have learned or received or heard from me, or seen in me—
put it into practice. And the God of peace will be with you.

Philippians 4:8–9 NIV

A Moment to Refresh

Continue in the things you have learned and become convinced of, knowing from whom you have learned them.

2 Timothy 3:14 NASB

❧

It's better to be wise than strong.

Proverbs 24:5 MSG

❧

If you are already wise, you will become even wiser. And if you are smart, you will learn to understand proverbs and sayings, as well as words of wisdom and all kinds of riddles.

Proverbs 1:5–6 CEV

❧

Do not be conformed to this world, but be transformed by the renewal of your mind, that by testing you may discern what is the will of God, what is good and acceptable and perfect.

Romans 12:2 ESV

❧

Instruct the wise, and they will be even wiser. Teach the righteous, and they will learn even more. Fear of the LORD is the foundation of wisdom. Knowledge of the Holy One results in good judgment.

Proverbs 9:9–10 NLT

Learning is not attained by chance. It must be sought for with ardor and attended to with diligence.

Abigail Adams

❧

Life is the soul's nursery—its training place for the destinies of eternity.

William Makepeace Thackeray

UNEXPECTED JOY

A Moment to Rest

Consider inviting someone over for an impromptu dinner. It doesn't have to be much. You don't need the right china or crystal, matching linens and napkins, or a gourmet meal. The accessories and the food that was served will be long forgotten, but the memory of a relaxing time with friends will linger far beyond the occasion.

Put aside thoughts of daily pressures or deadlines, or whether your house is clean enough for company. Just wear a welcoming smile. Remember, you're not simply entertaining; you are inviting someone in to feel valued and cared for, where relationships can be developed and nurtured. Your kitchen can be the place to iron out the world's wrinkles, a cozy room for small talk, or a safe haven for someone who needs to share a deep and secret hurt.

> *The beauty of the house is order; the blessing of the house is contentment. The glory of the house is hospitality. The crown of the house is godliness.*
>
> Author Unknown

And should your doorbell ring sometime when you think the house is a mess, you're not quite put together, or you haven't been to the grocery, answer it anyway. Welcome your friends, neighbors, and guests with a smile and a loving heart. Opening your home to unplanned visitors sometimes brings unexpected joys. Be grateful for the pleasure of being together.

A Moment to Reflect

*My dear friend, it is good that you help the brothers and
sisters, even those you do not know. . . . Please help them to
continue their trip in a way worthy of God.*

3 John 1:5–6 NCV

Caring enough to open your hand in hospitality opens
your heart as well. And as you take time to extend
yourself in your busy life, you will find the delight in
hospitality. You'll feel more caring, more gracious,
more warm and rested.

When you invite others for a quick cup of coffee or tea
or a bite to eat, you are modeling God's heart, his concern, and his kindness. You'll learn the joy of sharing
yourself. And when you get weary and need refresh-
ment, he is waiting to welcome you in the same way:
with warmth and love and total attention.

*Hospitality is a test for godliness because those who are self-
ish do not like strangers (especially needy ones) to intrude
upon their private lives. They prefer their own friends
who share their lifestyle. Only the humble have the
necessary resources to give of themselves to those
who could never give of themselves in return.*

Erwin Lutzer

*As you share your faith with others, I pray that they may
come to know all the blessings Christ has given us.*

Philemon 1:6 CEV

Let brotherly love continue. Do not forget to entertain strangers, for by so doing some have unwittingly entertained angels.

Hebrews 13:1–2 NKJV

❧

When God's people are in need, be ready to help them. Always be eager to practice hospitality.

Romans 12:13 NLT

❧

We ought therefore to show hospitality to such men so that we may work together for the truth.

3 John 1:8 NIV

❧

What we have seen and heard we also declare to you, so that you may have fellowship along with us.

1 John 1:3 HCSB

❧

Day by day continuing with one mind in the temple, and breaking bread from house to house, they were taking their meals together with gladness and sincerity of heart, praising God and having favor with all the people. And the Lord was adding to their number day by day those who were being saved.

Acts 2:46–47 NASB

Who practices hospitality entertains God himself.

Author Unknown

❧

If the world seems cold to you, kindle fires to warm it.

Lucy Larcom

FOCUSING ON GOD

A Moment to Rest

Meditating on Scripture is a great way to focus on God. Read one Bible verse. Take "God is love" (1 John 4:16 NIV), for starters. Close your eyes and think about each word. What picture does the word *God* bring to mind?

Next think about the word *is*. It may seem insignificant at first. Yet consider how the fact that God "is"—that he exists, that he's present, that he has no beginning or end—affects your life. How does the fact that "God is" affect your eternity? Now think about the word *love*. What type of actions does love bring to mind? How have you seen an invisible God's love visibly at work in the world?

Let us leave the surface and, without leaving the world, plunge into God.

Pierre Teilhard de Chardin

After you've spent a few minutes thinking about each word individually, concentrate on the whole phrase. Repeat it. What does it mean to you? What does it say about God? How does thinking about this Scripture draw you closer to God? How does it bring God's character into focus?

Some other verses that are good for this kind of meditation include "Love never fails" (1 Corinthians 13:8 NKJV), "Love one another" (John 15:12 NASB), and "Blessed are the peacemakers" (Matthew 5:9 ESV).

A Moment to Reflect

*I delight in Your commands, which I love. I will lift up
my hands to Your commands, which I love,
and will meditate on Your statutes.*

Psalm 119:47–48 HCSB

There is a type of meditation called *lectio divina*, which
is Latin for "divine reading." It is an ancient method of
focusing on God by meditating on Scripture.

It is important as you read larger passages of the Bible
to fully understand the context of a single verse. But
reading smaller passages will help to focus your
thoughts on a specific idea, and really see the details
you might have missed while reading the larger pas-
sage. Take time to linger over a single Scripture and
meditate on it. Each time you do, you will gain new
insight about God.

*It is no use to ask what those who love God do with Him.
There is no difficulty in spending our time with a friend we
love; our heart is always ready to open to Him; we do not
study what we shall say to Him, but it comes forth without
premeditation; we can keep nothing back—even if we have
nothing special to say, we like to be with Him.*

François Fénelon

❦

*Within your temple, O God, we meditate on your unfailing
love. Like your name, O God, your praise reaches
to the ends of the earth.*

Psalm 48:9–10 NIV

A Moment to Refresh

Devout meditation on the Word is more important to soul-health even than prayer. It is more needful for you to hear God's words than that God should hear yours, though the one will always lead to the other.

Frederick
Brotherton Meyer

❦

Meditation is like a needle after which comes a thread of gold, composed of affections, prayers and resolutions.

Alphonsus

I remember the days of old, I think about all your deeds, I meditate on the works of your hands.

Psalm 143:5 NRSV

❦

Help me understand the meaning of your commandments, and I will meditate on your wonderful deeds.

Psalm 119:27 NLT

❦

[Jesus said,] "You shall love the Lord your God with all your heart, and with all your soul, and with all your strength, and with all your mind."

Luke 10:27 NRSV

❦

*Let the words of my mouth
and the meditation of my heart
Be acceptable in Your sight,
O LORD, my strength and my Redeemer.*

Psalm 19:14 NKJV

❦

Do not let the Book of the Law depart from your mouth; meditate on it day and night, so that you can be careful to do everything written in it.

Joshua 1:8 NIV

TURNING PAGES

A Moment to Rest

Treat yourself to something good to read today. A story often seems to speak right to you. Books can be so gripping and the characters so appealing that you're a bit sad when you turn the last page. It can feel like you're saying good-bye to a friend.

Carry a paperback with you to help pass the time and stay relaxed even while standing in line or waiting for an appointment. Reading is also a great way to slow down and get away from the frantic day-to-day pace of your life. You can find inspiration in the pages that can calm your spirit when you need it the most. Much like making a new friend, deciding on something new to read offers the opportunity to challenge your mind, make you examine theories, or teach you lessons for life. Whatever your preference, books can create unlimited possibilities.

> *A book is like a garden carried in the pocket.*
>
> Ancient Proverb

The latest hardback offers a new world to conquer. What you read can inspire, inform, and delight you. Knowing something good to read is waiting at the end of your long day can make the anticipation so much the sweeter. Taking the time to turn a few pages is a reward to give yourself.

A Moment to Reflect

I have rejoiced in your laws as much as in riches.
I will study your commandments and reflect
on your ways. I will delight in your decrees
and not forget your word. . . . Open my eyes
to see the wonderful truths in your instructions.

Psalm 119:14–16, 18 NLT

Whatever you read for pleasure, also take time to read God's Word. He's written a book of letters just for you, packed with wisdom and truth. His book is full of promises for your future. If a problem or situation eludes a solution, ask God to direct you to his answers for you. Keep your heart attuned to God's desire for your life, and read prayerfully.

God's words will nourish you long after you close the book. Memorize your favorite passages and keep his words in your heart. They'll be there when you need them to cleanse your emotions, enlighten your mind, and wrap you in his confirming love.

I love old books
Frayed from pages turning.
Their warm, soft binding,
The words deftly planned.
They lead me through a story
Like a dear friend's hand.

Jan Coleman

Do not be conformed to this world, but be transformed by the renewing of your mind, that you may prove what is that good and acceptable and perfect will of God.

Romans 12:2 NKJV

The word of the LORD is right,
And all His work is done in truth.

Psalm 33:4 NKJV

❦

Pleasant words are a honeycomb,
Sweet to the soul.

Proverbs 16:24 NASB

❦

The wisdom from above is first pure,
then peace-loving, gentle, compliant,
full of mercy and good fruits,
without favoritism and hypocrisy.

James 3:17 HCSB

❦

I will remember the deeds of the LORD; yes,
I will remember your miracles of long ago.
I will meditate on all your works
and consider all your mighty deeds.

Psalm 77:11–12 NIV

❦

How much better it is to get wisdom than
gold! . . . Understanding is to be
chosen above silver.

Proverbs 16:16 NASB

Next to acquiring
good friends, the
best acquisition
is that of a
good book.

Charles Caleb
Colton

❦

A single line in the
Bible has consoled
me more than
all the books
I've ever read.

Immanuel Kant

A JAR OF GRATITUDE

A Moment to Rest

God answers prayer, and every prayer has an answer, though sometimes it may go unrecognized. Learn to distinguish his responses and give thanks for answered prayers. Recall some of the things you've prayed for during the past year. Place an empty jar and a pile of coins on the kitchen table while you're having your first cup of coffee.

There are four ways God answers prayer: No, not yet; No, I love you too much; Yes, I thought you'd never ask; Yes, and here's more.

Anne Lewis

Reflect on these questions: Were the answers what you expected? Are there some answers you're still waiting for? Are you glad God answered no to some prayers? Ask God to remind you of requests you may have forgotten. Place a coin in the jar with a prayer of gratitude each time you recognize God's answer to a specific petition.

The Bible describes how a pile of stones was used as a reminder of God's faithfulness. When God stopped the Jordan River so the Israelites could cross safely, stones from the dry riverbed were gathered into a pile on the opposite bank. This memorial helped future generations remember God's miraculous answer to prayer.

When you've finished reflecting on God's past and present gifts to you, leave the jar on the table and encourage others to also contribute coins to acknowledge their answered prayers.

A Moment to Reflect

Our LORD, I will sing of your love forever. Everyone yet to
be born will hear me praise your faithfulness. . . . "God's
love can always be trusted, and his faithfulness
lasts as long as the heavens."

Psalm 89:1–2 CEV

Having a visual reminder of God's faithfulness—
whether it's a jar of coins, an answered-prayer journal,
a scrapbook or diary, or even a pile of rocks in the
backyard—can encourage your faith. The reminder
serves as evidence that God cares about you, and keeping your reminder in a visible location will remind you
daily of how much you have.

Each time you pass the kitchen table and see your jar sitting there, pause for a moment and thank God for all he
has done for you and for those you love. When the jar is
full, use the coins to answer someone else's prayer.

New mercies, each returning day,
Hover around us while we pray;
New perils past, new sins forgiven,
New thoughts of God, new hopes of heaven.

John Keble

Give ear to my words, O LORD, consider my sighing. Listen
to my cry for help, my King and my God, for to you I pray.
In the morning, O LORD, you hear my voice; in the morning
I lay my requests before you and wait in expectation.

Psalm 5:1–3 NIV

A Moment to Refresh

We pray for silver, but God often gives us gold instead.

Martin Luther

❦

God never denied that soul anything that went as far as heaven to ask for it.

John Trapp

You answer our prayers. All of us must come to you.

Psalm 65:2 NLT

❦

[Jesus said,] "Whatever you ask for in prayer with faith, you will receive."

Matthew 21:22 NRSV

❦

The LORD has heard my plea for help; the LORD accepts my prayer.

Psalm 6:9 HCSB

❦

I love the LORD, because he has heard my voice and my pleas for mercy. Because he inclined his ear to me, therefore I will call on him as long as I live.

Psalm 116:1–2 ESV

❦

*Our God, you deserve praise in Zion, where we keep our promises to you. Everyone will come to you because you answer prayer. . . .
Our God, you save us, and your fearsome deeds answer our prayers for justice! You give hope to people everywhere on earth, even those across the sea.*

Psalm 65:1–2, 5 CEV

ESPECIALLY FOR YOU

A Moment to Rest

Isn't it amazing you came prepackaged with your own individual personality? You have unique gifts and abilities. Maybe you are a whiz at organizing or enjoy working with details that frustrate others. Maybe you are a people person and a natural leader.

In ancient times, talents were actually a form of money, but in Jesus' parable of the talents they represent the inborn resources given by God. The story begins with the master of an estate, about to leave on a journey, who entrusts his money to his servants, "each according to his ability." Each servant was expected to manage wisely what he had received. When the master returned a year later, he was pleased to find two of the servants had made good investments and doubled the money. But the third one trembled to confess, "I was afraid and hid your talent in the ground."

Our gifts are from God arranged by infinite wisdom, notes that make up the scores of creation's loftiest symphony, threads that compose the master tapestry of the universe.

A. W. Tozer

What are your gifts and abilities? Are you good with your hands? Do you have a knack for decorating? Do you have a good singing voice? Are you a good speaker? In your quiet time, ask God to show you how to multiply your talents so that you can serve God and others.

A Moment to Reflect

*Each has his own special gift from God, one of this kind
and one of another. . . . In whatever station or state or
condition of life each one was when he was called,
there let him continue with and close to God.*

1 Corinthians 7:7, 24 AMP

God has created a unique and special role for you to
play in this life. This role requires your specific talents,
your inborn personality, and all your experiences, the
bad as well as the good.

As you recognize the talents that you've been given,
you'll be even more eager to use them to serve God. As
you draw closer to God, be aware of the passions that
motivate you. See how they are partnered with your
gifts and abilities. Allow God to propel you into your
purpose, use your gifts, and experience joy as you
invest your talents for him.

*Use what talent you possess: the woods would be very
silent if no birds sang except those that sang best.*

Henry Van Dyke

❧

*Well done, good and faithful servant; you were faithful over a
few things, I will make you ruler over many things. Enter
into the joy of your lord. . . . For to everyone who has,
more will be given, and he will have abundance.*

Matthew 25:21, 29 NKJV

He has filled him with the Spirit of God, with skill, ability and knowledge in all kinds of crafts. . . . He has filled them with skill to do all kinds of work.

Exodus 35:31, 35 NIV

❧

God has given each of you a gift from his great variety of spiritual gifts. Use them well to serve one another. Do you have the gift of speaking? Then speak as though God himself were speaking through you. Do you have the gift of helping others? Do it with all the strength and energy that God supplies. Then everything you do will bring glory to God through Jesus Christ.

1 Peter 4:10–11 NLT

❧

According to the grace given to us, we have different gifts.

Romans 12:6 HCSB

❧

God doesn't take back the gifts he has given or forget about the people he has chosen.

Romans 11.29 CEV

To be granted some kind of usable talent and to be able to use it to the fullest extent of which you are capable — this to me, is a kind of joy that is almost unequaled.

Lawrence Welk

❧

God's gifts put man's best dreams to shame.

Elizabeth Barrett Browning

TRIVIAL PURSUITS

A Moment to Rest

Do you feel overextended, as though you are always dashing in different directions? Do you often feel like a tumbleweed being tossed from here to there? Does there constantly seem to be another objective, another goal, another task, another commitment? Does it seem like you will never finish all you've set out to accomplish? Do you have to juggle and change your priorities? If you said yes to any of these questions, now is the time to find a quiet corner, sit down with pencil and paper, and make a list. Title it "Trivial Pursuits."

> *Tell me to what you pay attention, and I will tell you who you are.*
>
> José Ortega y Gasset

Ask yourself: What are the things that are taking up my precious time? Are they really important? Do I neglect the relationships that really matter? Do I spend time on things that nurture me, please God, and enhance my relationship with him, or on doing things that don't really count in the long run?

Identify the nonessential tasks that drain your time and plan now to trim them from your life. Try to bring balance and order to your life by spending time on activities that will help you be a whole person. Seek fulfillment of God's purpose for you in everything you do.

A Moment to Reflect

*I once thought these things were valuable, but now I
consider them worthless because of what Christ
has done. . . . For his sake I have discarded
everything else . . . so that I could gain Christ.*

Philippians 3:7–8 NLT

In God's opinion, the small and meaningful things are
worth more than the trivial pursuits of life. Trivial things
can bring disorder and exhaustion. Invest your time
wisely. Take time for yourself and time to get to know
God. As you do, the Lord will speak to you in a gentle
way that speaks specifically to your heart. He will lovingly show you what's truly necessary, what goals are worth
pursuing, and what qualities of character make for real
happiness. He will give you the calming joy that comes
from being in harmony with your life.

*Earthly treasures won't stand the test,
For in time, moth and rust will destroy.
Come with me, to your place of rest,
In my presence, there's fullness of joy.
A shelter where trials of life will cease,
Through the comfort of my love divine.
Where I quietly whisper into the peace,
"I am yours, won't you please be mine?"*

Sylvia Lavallée

*Seek first the kingdom of God and his righteousness,
and all these things will be added to you.*

Matthew 6:33 ESV

A Moment to Refresh

At the end of life, you will never regret not having passed one more test, not winning one more verdict, not closing one more deal. You will regret time not spent with a husband, a child, a friend, a parent.

Barbara Bush

✿

Take glory in neither money, if you have some, nor in influential friends, but in God who gives you everything and above all wants to give you himself.

Thomas à Kempis

[Jesus said,] "Do not store up for yourselves treasures on earth, where moth and rust destroy, and where thieves break in and steal. But store up for yourselves treasures in heaven, where moth and rust do not destroy, and where thieves do not break in and steal. For where your treasure is, there your heart will be also."

Matthew 6:19–21 NIV

✿

Your beauty should come from within you—the beauty of a gentle and quiet spirit that will never be destroyed and is very precious to God.

1 Peter 3:4 NCV

✿

Make me want to obey you, rather than to be rich. Take away my foolish desires, and let me find life by walking with you.

Psalm 119:36–37 CEV

✿

A good name is to be more desired than great wealth,
Favor is better than silver and gold.

Proverbs 22:1 NASB

A HEARTFELT THANK~YOU

A Moment to Rest

Take out a sheet of your best writing paper. Or, if you prefer, sit down at your computer. It's time to write a heartfelt thank-you note. You won't need any postage, and your spelling won't be checked. This note is headed straight for heaven.

Listing everything God has given you would take a lifetime. So limit this note to the number one thing for which you are grateful. It's easy to simply say a quick thank-you to God via prayer, but you can better explore the depth of your gratitude if you write out a note of appreciation the same way you would write to a friend who touched your heart with unexpected kindness.

God is always meeting the needs of all of His children.

Edward Miller

Think how having this has changed your life, how it has encouraged your heart, and how it has met an individual need or desire. Consider what life would be like without it. As you're finishing up, add a paragraph listing all the things you are grateful for today—especially those you might easily overlook. Put the finished note into an envelope addressed to My Heavenly Father and keep it in your Bible. Open and read it anytime you are facing a discouraging day.

A Moment to Reflect

Good people will have rich blessings. . . . Good people will
be remembered as a blessing. . . . The words of a good
person give life, like a fountain of water. . . .
Good people are rewarded with life.

Proverbs 10:6–7, 11, 16 NCV

When a friend goes out of her way for you, it's natural to thank her and brag to others about what she's done. Think about doing the same thing with God. Freely share what God has done in your life. Your words may help others recognize his hand at work in their own lives, and encourage them to thank God along with you.

The things we are given are best shared, both verbally and physically. When God's gifts bring about an abundance of material resources, use them to help others. It may be why God brought the gift your way in the first place.

An easy thing, O Power Divine,
To thank thee for these gifts of Thine,
For summer's sunshine, winter's snow,
For hearts that kindle, thoughts that glow;
But when shall I attain to this —
To thank Thee for the things I miss?

Thomas Wentworth Higginson

❦

The same Lord is Lord of all and richly blesses all
who call on him, for, "Everyone who calls on the
name of the Lord will be saved."

Romans 10:12–13 NIV

*God will fully satisfy every need of yours
according to his riches in glory in Christ Jesus.*

Philippians 4:19 NRSV

[The] faithful . . . will abound with blessings.

Proverbs 28:20 NASB

*The LORD gives his people strength.
The LORD blesses them with peace.*

Psalm 29:11 NLT

*The LORD will bless you if you respect him and
obey his laws. . . . You will be happy
and all will go well.*

Psalm 128:1–2 CEV

*Blessed be the God and Father of our LORD
Jesus Christ, who has blessed us with every
spiritual blessing in the heavens, in Christ.*

Ephesians 1:3 HCSB

*Every good thing given and every perfect gift is
from above, coming down from the Father of
lights, with whom there is no variation
or shifting shadow.*

James 1:17 NASB

*O Thou who hast
given us so much,
mercifully grant
us one more
thing — a grateful
heart.*

George Herbert

*Now let the soul
number its gains
and count its
treasures. They
are so fine that
they refine the
hands which
count them.*

Phillips Brooks

UNSINKABLE OPTIMISM

A Moment to Rest

Five days into a trip across the Atlantic on the legendary *Titanic*, Margaret Tobin Brown found herself bobbing around in a lifeboat in the freezing cold with fourteen other women and a prophet-of-doom officer. The officer insisted they'd never escape the undertow when the ship went down.

> *Your living is determined not so much by what life brings to you as by the attitude you bring to life; not so much by what happens to you as by the way your mind looks at what happens.*
>
> John Homer Miller

Margaret refused to give in to negative thinking. If this man wasn't going to save the lifeboat, she would. She insisted they keep warm by fast-paced rowing during those daunting hours before they were rescued, and lifted their hopes with her indomitable spirit. She created survivor lists and radioed them to the families. She even raised money for destitute victims of the sinking, collecting almost $10,000 in pledges. She rightly earned her famous nickname, "The Unsinkable Molly Brown."

Place a note on the refrigerator to remind you that with God all things are possible. Take a moment to thank God for his gifts of hope and optimism. Feel your spirits immediately rise.

A Moment to Reflect

*Give thanks to the LORD and pray to him. Tell the nations
what he has done. Sing to him; sing praises to him. Tell
about all his miracles. Be glad that you are his; let those
who seek the LORD be happy. Depend on the LORD and his
strength; always go to him for help. Remember the
miracles he has done, his wonders, and his decisions.*

1 Chronicles 16:8–12 NCV

If you're uncertain about something today and find
yourself starting to slip into negative thinking, make it a
point to zero in on the positive. If you can't see through
the fog, if your future is fuzzy and dim, now is a great
opportunity to practice being optimistic.

If you're overwhelmed with doubt, remember that God
wants to give you a buoyant spirit to rise above any circumstance, no matter how dark and difficult things
seem at the present time. When you place your confidence in God, you are secure in the hope of your Savior.
With him at your side, you, too, will be unsinkable.

*The more faith you have,
The more you believe,
The more goals you set
The more you'll achieve.
Remember no matter
How futile things seem,
With faith, there is no
Impossible dream!*

Alice Joyce Davidson

A Moment to Refresh

A happy person is not a person in a certain set of circumstances, but rather a person with a certain set of attitudes.

Hugh Downs

❀

The way in which you endure that which you must endure is more important than the crisis itself.

Sam Rutigliano

[Love] always protects, always trusts, always hopes, always perseveres. Love never fails.

1 Corinthians 13:7–8 NIV

❀

Worry weighs us down;
a cheerful word picks us up.

Proverbs 12:25 MSG

❀

We put our hope in the LORD.
He is our help and our shield.
In him our hearts rejoice,
for we trust in his holy name.
Let your unfailing love surround us, LORD,
for our hope is in you alone.

Psalm 33:20–22 NLT

❀

Your great love reaches to the skies,
your truth to the clouds.

Psalm 57:10 NCV

❀

A joyful heart is good medicine.

Proverbs 17:22 HCSB

BASKING IN BUBBLES

A Moment to Rest

Get up a little early and begin your day with a bubble bath. Schedule time in the tub on a Saturday afternoon. Or substitute watching the evening news with basking in bubbles glistening by candlelight.

You don't have to wait until nightfall. Take a little private time for yourself whenever the house is finally quiet. When it comes to relaxation and restoration, time in the tub is well spent. Light a solitary candle and step into something more comfortable—a tub filled with warm, soothing water topped with a froth of fragrant bubble bath, beads, salts, or oil.

> *With joy you will draw water from the wells of salvation.*
>
> Isaiah 12:3 NRSV

If finding uninterrupted time isn't possible at the moment, enjoy a "dry run" in your mind. Close your eyes and imagine the sound of running water, the sweet floral scent of your favorite bath fragrance, and lots of bubbles. Picture the bubbles multiplying as the water rises. Step into that tub. Feel the warm water as it makes your muscles relax and your cares dissolve.

As you relax in the tub or just in your mind, spend a few moments confessing to God any areas where you feel you have fallen short. Then, relax in the warm comfort of God's cleansing forgiveness.

A Moment to Reflect

Keep your heart with all diligence,
For out of it spring the issues of life.

Proverbs 4:23 NKJV

One of the beauties of a bubble bath is that you can get clean without scrubbing. In the same way, a squeaky clean spirit isn't something you have to work at. Inner purity is a gift from God.

Relaxing in a bubble bath is a good time to cleanse your inner heart and mind as well as your body. When you drain the tub, picture all the mistakes you've made, the wrong choices, the things you wish you had done differently, going down the drain along with the dirty water. Enjoy the feeling of being wholly clean.

Oh! To be clean as a mountain river!
Clean as the air above the clouds,
or on the middle seas!
As the throbbing ether that fills the gulf
between star and star!
Nay, as the thought of the Son of Man Himself.

George MacDonald

❧

Sincerity and truth are what you require; fill my mind with
your wisdom. Remove my sin, and I will be clean; wash me,
and I will be whiter than snow. Let me hear the sounds of joy
and gladness. . . . Create a pure heart in me, O God,
and put a new and loyal spirit in me.

Psalm 51:6–8, 10 GNT

When the kindness and love of God our Savior
appeared, he saved us, not because of righteous
things we had done, but because of his mercy.
He saved us through the washing of rebirth
and renewal by the Holy Spirit.

Titus 3:4–5 NIV

❧

Let's come near God with pure hearts and a
confidence that comes from having faith. Let's
keep our hearts pure, our consciences free from
evil, and our bodies washed with clean water.

Hebrews 10:22 CEV

❧

[Jesus said,] "First clean the inside of the cup,
so that the outside also may become clean."

Matthew 23:26 NRSV

❧

What God has made clean,
do not call common.

Acts 10:15 ESV

❧

Just as water mirrors your face,
so your face mirrors your heart.

Proverbs 27:19 MSG

Prayer is the inner
bath of love into
which the soul
plunges itself.

Jean-Baptiste
Marie Vianney

❧

Plenteous grace
with Thee is
found, grace to
cover all my sins;
let the healing
streams abound,
make and keep me
pure within.

Charles Wesley

YOU DESERVE IT

A Moment to Rest

Find some time to pamper yourself. In Ecclesiastes, Solomon says to enjoy to the fullest the life that God has given. Recognize and enjoy the fruits of your labor as another of God's wonderful gifts. It is a good thing and you deserve it.

> *I decided there is nothing better than to enjoy food and drink and to find satisfaction in work. Then I realized that these pleasures are from the hand of God.*
>
> Ecclesiastes 2:24
> NLT

The dictionary defines *pamper* in this way: "to be indulgent with, to coddle, to spoil." As a woman, you may cringe at the thought of spoiling, of giving in too much to a child's impulses. You know that many a character has been ruined by a lenient parent. But you aren't a child; you are a woman. Indulging in the occasional pampering can refresh and prepare you to meet the complex demands on your time.

So how do you want to pamper yourself today? You could splurge on a new hairstyle or buy some real maple syrup for your pancakes. What about picking up that new outfit you looked at last week, or treating yourself to a day out with some girlfriends for lunch and a movie? Spoil yourself by doing something that will make you smile, make you stop and say, "Now, that was really worth it!"

A Moment to Reflect

Praise the LORD and do not forget all his kindnesses. . . .
The LORD does what is right and fair for all who are
wronged by others. . . . The LORD shows mercy and is
kind. He does not become angry quickly,
and he has great love.

Psalm 103:2, 6, 8 NCV

God wants to hold nothing back from you. He's pleased when you take time for yourself to buy something special or to have a little fun. He knows you deserve all the enjoyable things that come your way. God wants to add to your inner beauty, your outer usefulness, and your gladness.

As you pamper yourself, your daily work has more meaning and purpose. It helps keep your world in better balance. God provides both work and pleasure as ways to serve him. Enjoy life to the fullest, and be constantly aware that all comes from his hand.

Live while you live, the Epicure would say,
And seize the pleasures of the present day;
Live while you live, the sacred preacher cries,
And give to God each moment as it flies;
Lord, in my view let both united be;
I live in pleasure when I live to thee.

Phillip Doddridge

❦

Each day that we live, he provides for our needs
and gives us the strength of a young eagle.

Psalm 103:5 CEV

A Moment to Refresh

Freedom means I have been set free to become all that God wants me to be, to achieve all that God wants me to achieve, to enjoy all that God wants me to enjoy.

Warren Wiersbe

⁂

I asked God for all things so I could enjoy life. He gave me life so I could enjoy all things.

Author Unknown

Of His fullness we have all received, and grace for grace.

John 1:16 NKJV

⁂

You reveal the path of life to me; in Your presence is abundant joy; in Your right hand are eternal pleasures.

Psalm 16:11 HCSB

⁂

As grace extends to more and more people it may increase thanksgiving, to the glory of God.

2 Corinthians 4:15 ESV

⁂

[God] has shown kindness by giving you rain from heaven and crops in their seasons; he provides you with plenty of food and fills your hearts with joy.

Acts 14:17 NIV

⁂

This is what I want you to do: Ask the Father for whatever is in keeping with the things I've revealed to you. Ask in my name, according to my will, and he'll most certainly give it to you. Your joy will be a river overflowing its banks!

John 16:23–24 MSG

KEEP IT SIMPLE

A Moment to Rest

You can find freedom in clearing out clutter. So today, instead of pondering, you're going to be purging your possessions.

Head for your bedroom closet. Ask God for joy in the job ahead. Pray for wisdom in deciding what to let go of and what to hold on to. Then start the sorting process.

As you gather clothes you no longer need or wear—the dress that's too big, the sweater that's too tight, the robe you haven't worn in a year, and the shoes that don't match anything— think of each item as a stone you're preparing to skim across a mountain lake. Don't just drop your clothes into a pile, toss them several feet away.

> *Clutter is what happens to things when they become useless but friendly.*
>
> Russell Lynes

Imagine the sound of the stone breaking the water's surface. Picture the ripples emanating from its point of entry across the lake. Before continuing, enjoy the soothing image of your stone sinking to its watery resting place.

Then carefully fold each of your discards, clean them if needed, and place them in a bag to donate to charity. Enjoy the breathing room you've made in your closet and plan the next place to purge. Feel the freedom of having less clutter in your life.

A Moment to Reflect

For everything there is a season . . . a time to lose; a time to keep, and a time to cast away.

Ecclesiastes 3:1, 6 ESV

Every piece of clothing comes with a price. That price has to do with money, of course, but the price is also that of time and attention. Every item you have to take care of and the more clutter that fills your life and closets, the less time, energy, and resources you have to give to family and others. Purchasing, laundering, dusting, shopping, scrubbing, repairing, and discarding are simply more time commitments you have to squeeze out of your busy schedule.

Keep it simple. At least twice a year, ask God for wisdom in getting rid of any "stones" you've accumulated. Donate unneeded items to charities for use in helping others. The less clutter you have to care for, the less there will be to distract you from what's really important. You'll find you have much more time to spend with God, your family, and others who play a significant part in your life.

Whatever we have of this world in our hands, our care must be to keep it out of our hearts, lest it come between us and Christ.

Matthew Henry

❧

*A wise woman strengthens her family. . . .
Being kind to the needy brings happiness.*

Proverbs 14:1, 21 NCV

As goods increase, so do those who consume them. And what benefit are they to the owner except to feast his eyes on them?

Ecclesiastes 5:11 NIV

❦

I know how to live on almost nothing or with everything. I have learned the secret of living in every situation.

Philippians 4:12 NLT

❦

Godliness with contentment is great gain. For we brought nothing into this world, and it is certain we can carry nothing out.

1 Timothy 6:6–7 NKJV

❦

Keep your lives free from the love of money and be content with what you have, because God has said, "Never will I leave you; never will I forsake you."

Hebrews 13:5 NIV

❦

[Jesus said,] "Take care! Protect yourself against the least bit of greed. Life is not defined by what you have, even when you have a lot."

Luke 12:15 MSG

Simplicity is making the journey of this life with just baggage enough.

Charles Dudley Warner

❦

The ability to simplify means to eliminate the unnecessary so that the necessary may speak.

Hans Hofmann

STAIRWAY TO HEAVEN

A Moment to Rest

Do you need comfort, reassurance, or guidance right now? Go to a quiet spot and immerse yourself in prayer. You don't have to be eloquent, just sincere. Come to him just as you are. Just be yourself. Jesus said, "God knows what is in your heart."

> *Real prayer is simply being in the presence of God. . . . I just want to be with him for a time, to feel his comradeship, his concern, his caring around me and about me, and then to go out to a world warmer because I spent an hour with him.*
>
> William Barclay

Close your mind to everything around you and open your heart. You can start by praying the Lord's Prayer. Between each verse, pause for a while, savor the peace and quiet, and feel the holy presence of God deep within you. Then pour out your heart to him. He is listening.

As you speak the prayer, bring all your needs before him. Be candid; you can lay all your concerns before God; he will understand all your desires, yearnings, and feelings. God does not tire of hearing the sound of your heart expressing its deepest feelings.

Then give God a gift for being there to listen to you; tell him to work in your heart as he chooses. His will, not yours. Don't try to imagine what he'll do or how he'll work out the details. Simply seek his presence.

A Moment to Reflect

In the morning, having risen a long while before
daylight, He went out and departed to a
solitary place; and there He prayed.

Mark 1:35 NKJV

Prayer is the stairway to heaven, a climb that leads to the treasures of God's mercies and the promise of eternal life. Your prayers link you to God and allow you to sense his presence and get to know him intimately.

When you speak honestly in your own voice, holding nothing back, God becomes your trusted friend. You love and enjoy him just because he is there with you. Pray with a believing heart, and your relationship with God will deepen and mature. Your inner spirit will be at peace. The hearts and minds of those who pray are confident and peaceful.

When I feel still and very empty
I try to turn my thoughts to prayer,
A little light turns on inside
And suddenly My God is there.
My doubts come from their stony places,
He turns each one into a flower,
My heart gets into heaven's gate,
I'm linked again with Him in prayer.

Marion Schoeberlein

A Moment to Refresh

A prayer in its simplest definition is merely a wish turned Godward.

Phillips Brooks

❀

Prayer is like the turning of an electric switch. It does not create the current; it simply provides a channel through which the electric current may flow.

Max Handel

Do not be anxious about anything, but in everything, by prayer and petition, with thanksgiving, present your requests to God. And the peace of God, which transcends all understanding, will guard your hearts and your minds in Christ Jesus.

Philippians 4:6–7 NIV

❀

God did listen! He paid attention to my prayer. Praise God, who did not ignore my prayer or withdraw his unfailing love from me.

Psalm 66:19–20 NLT

❀

The LORD has heard my cry for help; The LORD will answer my prayer.

Psalm 6:9 NCV

❀

God answered their prayers because they trusted him.

1 Chronicles 5:20 MSG

❀

[Jesus said,] "Whatever you ask in prayer, believe that you have received it, and it will be yours. And whenever you stand praying, forgive, if you have anything against anyone, so that your Father also who is in heaven may forgive you your trespasses."

Mark 11:24–25 ESV

PRAISE GOD

A Moment to Rest

Step away for a few minutes from all the earthly things that clamor for your attention and look upward. Praise God for the good things he has placed in your life—the people you treasure, your health, your home, the food on your table. Nothing lifts a woman's spirit more than the simple act of praising God.

When you express your admiration by words or actions, you are reconnecting on a deep level with your Creator, through whom you have access to all you could ever want or need. If you are in a place where it is appropriate, speak the words out loud to settle them deeply in your heart.

> *You awaken us to delight in your praise; for you have made us for yourself, and our hearts are restless until they find their rest in you.*
>
> Augustine of Hippo

Now speak words of praise to God for who he is—loving, kind, just, and blameless. Of course your words can never fully encompass the greatness of God. He is greater and more wonderful than any human mind can comprehend. Praise him for those qualities you appreciate most.

When you have finished your praising, linger for a few more moments in God's presence. The Bible says that when God's people praise him, he is always there with them. Let him strengthen and inspire you.

A Moment to Reflect

May your glorious name be praised! May it be exalted above all blessing and praise! You alone are the LORD. You made the skies and the heavens and all the stars. You made the earth and the seas and everything in them. You preserve them all, and all the angels of heaven worship you.

Nehemiah 9:5–6 NLT

Praising God is to the spirit what regular exercise is to the body. It strengthens and invigorates. That isn't just because he is worthy of your praise. It is also because praising God helps you to remember that he is bigger than any situation you may be facing—bigger than any personal failure or frustration you may have experienced.

Take the time to praise God. Open your mind, your heart, and your spirit to the renewal that only he can give. When you do, you will find that one of the greatest consequences of praising God is that you will want to praise him even more. And each time you praise him you will be drawing down even more blessed benefits for yourself.

Let us, with a gladsome mind,
Praise the Lord, for he is kind:
For his mercies aye endure,
Ever faithful, ever sure.

John Milton

The LORD is my strength and shield. I trust him, and he helps me. I am very happy, and I praise him with my song.

Psalm 28:7 NCV

Enter into His gates with thanksgiving, And into His courts with praise. Be thankful to Him, and bless His name.

Psalm 100:4 NKJV

Sing to him, sing praise to him; tell of all his wonderful acts. Glory in his holy name; let the hearts of those who seek the LORD rejoice.

Psalm 105:2–3 NIV

Praise the LORD! Oh give thanks to the LORD, for He is good; For His lovingkindness is everlasting.

Psalm 106:1 NASB

I praise you, for I am fearfully and wonderfully made. Wonderful are your works; that I know very well.

Psalm 139:14 NRSV

The worship of God is not a rule of safety—it is an adventure of the spirit.

Alfred North Whitehead

Worship is the celebration of life in its totality.

William Stringfellow

Express Yourself

A Moment to Rest

The Victorian woman of the 1800s was trained to have gracious manners and go to great lengths to remain feminine. Her tightly drawn corset ensured a shapely waist in satin gowns with balloon sleeves and billowing hoop skirts. An elegant hostess, she was often called the "angel in the house." Tea was served in her finest bone china on a lace-covered table. Proper ladies would not be so immodest, of course, to discuss delicate, private matters. Women were not expected to have strong opinions, and they were not encouraged to explore opportunities outside the home.

> *A thing of beauty*
> *is a joy forever;*
> *Its loveliness*
> *increases;*
> *It will never pass*
> *into nothingness.*
>
> John Keats

Things have changed. Many women today dress in jeans or casual skirts or pants around the house and at work. They drink from whatever mug they find in the cabinet. They're not so shy about speaking candidly. You can still express your femininity. You're a special woman.

What makes you feel feminine? Do you like soft colors, a special perfume, a delicate piece of jewelry? Do you love fresh flowers on the table, sipping exotic tea from a china cup, or luxuriating in a scented bubble bath? Incorporate something delicate into your life this week. Experiment. Enjoy your femininity in your own personal way.

A Moment to Reflect

All beautiful you are, my darling;
there is no flaw in you.

Song of Solomon 4:7 NIV

God rejoices in your womanhood. The Bible celebrates feminine beauty. Tuck this truth in your heart—the Lord sees you as a "garden spring, a well of flowing water" (Song of Solomon 4:15 HCSB). God rejoices in the splendor of your womanhood, and he gave it to you as a gift to be cultivated. He wants you to celebrate being a woman and to make the most of the qualities he has given you. As you recognize, appreciate, and express the gift God has given you, savor the deep satisfaction that comes with feeling at home with your femininity. Enjoy the confidence he gives you in being a woman who knows who she is, what she wants in life, and how with God's help she will reach her goals. Delight in God's company as you nurture and cherish the woman he's made you to be.

As The Holy Master Potter,
With His love, so patiently,
Unfolds my spirit like a rose,
He reveals the beauty in me.
His vessel of pure loveliness,
Now shines in brilliant light,
A woman of great worth,
In whom, God can delight.

Sylvia Lavallée

A Moment to Refresh

*She's a woman beyond compare. My dove is
perfection, pure and innocent as the day she was
born. . . . Everyone . . . blessed and praised her.
"Has anyone ever seen anything like this —
dawn-fresh, moon-lovely, sun-radiant, ravish-
ing as the night sky with its galaxies of stars?"*

Song of Solomon 6:9–10 MSG

*True strength is
delicate.*

Louise Nevelson

*You should clothe yourselves instead with the
beauty that comes from within, the unfading
beauty of a gentle and quiet spirit,
which is so precious to God.*

1 Peter 3:4–5 NLT

*Honor women!
They entwine and
weave heavenly
roses in our
earthly life.*

Johann Christoph
Von Schiller

*O my dove, in the clefts of the rock,
in the secret place of the steep pathway,
Let me see your form,
Let me hear your voice;
For your voice is sweet,
And your form is lovely.*

Song of Solomon 2:14 NASB

*Your lips are like a strand of scarlet,
And your mouth is lovely.*

Song of Solomon 4:3 NKJV

SELAH

A Moment to Rest

A good novel can get your adrenaline going, leading you to turn pages faster and faster. Poetry can have the opposite effect. It slows you down. It makes you stop, think, question, and reflect.

Begin by reading Psalm 143:5-6: "I remember the days of long ago; I meditate on all your works and consider what your hands have done.

I spread out my hands to you; my soul thirsts for you like a parched land. *Selah*" (NIV).

This may not look like the poetry you're accustomed to. It doesn't include measured stanzas or patterns of rhyme. Psalms are poems filled with raw emotion and metaphor. Originally written to be sung as a form of worship, some of them include musical terms, like *selah*.

> *Poetry is the spontaneous overflow of powerful feelings: it takes its origin from emotion recollected in tranquility.*
>
> William Wordsworth

Selah means "pause." During this pause, people would listen to a musical interlude or simply reflect on what had been sung. *Selah* was a moment of inner rest written directly into the poem. So *selah* right now. Reread the words above. Picture yourself as a solitary woman in a parched land. How does God quench your thirst? Stop, think, question, reflect on the beautiful poetry of the Psalms, and pray.

A Moment to Reflect

My heart overflows with a beautiful thought! . . . For my tongue is like the pen of a skillful poet.

Psalm 45:1 NLT

Reading through Psalms is one way to immerse yourself in great poetry, and work a little *selah* into your daily schedule. If you read a psalm a day, you'll have read three months worth of prayer-provoking poetry when you're finished.

Try reading one each morning—before your day gets hectic. Remind yourself to be the real you when you talk to God, the way the psalmists were. Pay attention to the emotions expressed in each psalm and the honesty with which they are voiced, whether joy, anger, despair, or praise. Don't forget to *selah* as you read.

Could we with ink the ocean fill,
And were the heavens of parchment made,
Were every stalk on earth a quill,
And every man a scribe by trade,
To write the love of God above
Would drain the ocean dry,
Nor could the scroll contain the whole,
Though stretch'd from sky to sky.

"*Chaldee Ode*," translated by
Rabbi Mayir Ben Isaac

❧

The right word spoken at the right time is as beautiful as gold apples in a silver bowl.

Proverbs 25:11 NCV

Tremble, and do not sin;
Meditate in your heart upon your bed,
and be still. Selah.

Psalm 4:4 NASB

❦

You are my hiding place;
You shall preserve me from trouble;
You shall surround me with
songs of deliverance. Selah

Psalm 32:7 NKJV

❦

Trust in him at all times, O people; pour out
your heart before him; God is a refuge for us.
Selah

Psalm 62:8 ESV

❦

You, O LORD, are a shield around me, my
glory, and the one who lifts up my head. I cry
aloud to the LORD, and he answers me
from his holy hill. Selah

Psalm 3:3–4 NRSV

❦

Who is He, this King of glory? The LORD of
Hosts, He is the King of glory. Selah

Psalm 24:10 HCSB

A poem is the very
image of life
expressed in its
eternal truth.

Percy Bysshe
Shelley

❦

The psychological
mechanism used
by grace to raise
us to prayer is the
same that puts in
movement the
poetic experience.

Henri Bremond

TOMORROW IS ANOTHER DAY

A Moment to Rest

Gone With the Wind is the unforgettable story by Margaret Mitchell. It sold more than fifty thousand copies on the first day of its release in 1936. Scarlett O'Hara, a fiery young Southern belle with the world at her plantation doorstep, encounters a war that changes her country and her life. She emerges strong and determined, but due to a misplaced dream and some hasty and foolish decisions, Scarlett misses her chance at true happiness.

It's never too late — in fiction or in life — to revise.

Nancy Thayer

Why has this story captured the minds of millions? Is it the struggle of a society to rise from the ashes of destruction, or is it because of the immortal hope expressed by Scarlett in the last line of the book: "After all, tomorrow is another day"?

Most people have regrets and dwell on what they perceive as failures and missed opportunities. That's why stories like Scarlett's have such timeless appeal. There is a need for a refuge like Tara to examine one's life, lick one's wounds, learn one's lessons, and have another chance to plan and make things right. Everyone wants a place where endings are happy, dreams come true, and Rhett comes home.

A Moment to Reflect

*Oh, the joys of those who . . . delight in doing everything
the LORD wants. . . . They are like trees
planted along the riverbank, bearing fruit each
season without fail. Their leaves never wither,
and in all they do, they prosper.*

Psalm 1:1–3 NLT

Whenever your failures fly through your mind, keep in mind that failure is not the same as defeat in God's plan. What could seem like an ending may really be a new beginning, for God gives second chances. God uses your fumbles to redirect your life, remold your goals, and reveal your priorities. He'll renew your spirit and let you triumph.

The name Tara refers to a hill in ancient Ireland, the royal seat of the Celtic high kings. When you're discouraged, just withdraw to your own Tara, in God's arms, and let him grant you a fresh start.

*Things in the past,
Are dead and gone,
Leave them behind,
Then just move on.
Yesterday is history,
Tomorrow is a mystery,
Today is God's gift to me,
To make it all that it can be.*

Sylvia Lavallée

A Moment to Refresh

If you have made mistakes . . . there is always another chance for you. You may have a fresh start any moment you choose, for this thing we call "failure" is not the falling down, but the staying down.

Mary Pickford

❧

What becomes of lost opportunities? Perhaps our guardian angel gathers them up and will give them back when we've grown wiser—and will use them rightly.

Helen Keller

Do not remember the former things, Nor consider the things of old. Behold, I will do a new thing, Now it shall spring forth; Shall you not know it?

Isaiah 43:18–19 NKJV

❧

This I call to mind and therefore I have hope: Because of the LORD's great love we are not consumed, for his compassions never fail. They are new every morning; great is your faithfulness.

Lamentations 3:21–23 NIV

❧

Do your work willingly, as though you were serving the Lord himself, and not just your earthly master. In fact, the Lord Christ is the one you are really serving, and you know that he will reward you.

Colossians 3:23–24 CEV

❧

You will forget your trouble. . . . And darkness will seem like morning.

Job 11:16–17 NCV

❧

You keep me going when times are tough—my bedrock, GOD, since my childhood.

Psalm 71:5 MSG

DEEPEST DESIRES

A Moment to Rest

It's time to quiet your mind and listen to your inner longings. Even if you haven't had the time or the solitude to pay attention to them in a while, they're still there, painting your dreams and whispering hope into your heart. Find a spot where you can get comfortable, and bring along a pencil and paper.

Pay attention to what comes to mind as you ponder the question: What do I long for?

Write down your deepest longings. At first, what you write might seem a little like a Christmas wish list. But delve deeper. Behind that longing for a carpool-free day may be a desire for more personal freedom—or it could be your body's exhausted cry for some extended downtime. Turn your longing list into a time of prayer. God already knows the deepest desires of your heart.

> *What oxygen is to the lungs, such is hope for the meaning of life.*
>
> Heinrich Emil Brunner

Finish by asking God for the courage to hope. It takes a believing heart to keep moving forward with joy while at the same time carrying unfulfilled longings.

Be open to God satisfying your yearnings in unexpected ways in his own time. Then keep your eyes open for his answers to your deepest needs.

A Moment to Reflect

You will forget your misery; it will be like water flowing
away. Your life will be brighter than the noonday. Even
darkness will be as bright as morning.
Having hope will give you courage. You will
be protected and will rest in safety.

Job 11:16–18 NLT

The pursuit of happiness cannot meet your deepest desires. Only God can do that. Wealth, success, and popularity may feel satisfying for a while, but people who rely on things like these to fill their longings will never be satisfied ultimately.

In that respect, having unfulfilled longings is a good thing. God uses these longings to point people to him, because at the heart of every deep desire lies a longing for something that only God can give. Knowing you have access to gifts such as unconditional love, forgiveness, peace, and eternal life is the only unshakable source of hope.

Behind the clouds the starlight lurks,
Through showers the sunbeams fall;
For God, who loveth all His works,
Has left His hope for all.

John Greenleaf Whittier

We who have fled for refuge . . . have strong encouragement
to hold fast to the hope set before us. We have this as a sure
and steadfast anchor of the soul, a hope that enters into the
inner place behind the curtain, where Jesus has
gone as a forerunner on our behalf.

Hebrews 6:18–20 ESV

May the God of hope fill you with all joy and peace in believing, so that you may abound in hope by the power of the Holy Spirit.

Romans 15:13 NRSV

❧

Only God gives inward peace, and I depend on him. . . . Trust God, my friends, and always tell him each one of your concerns.

Psalm 62:5, 8 CEV

❧

"I know the plans I have for you," declares the LORD, "plans to prosper you and not to harm you, plans to give you hope and a future."

Jeremiah 29:11 NIV

❧

Hope does not disappoint, because the love of God has been poured out within our hearts through the Holy Spirit who was given to us.

Romans 5:5 NASB

❧

Faith is the substance of things hoped for, the evidence of things not seen.

Hebrews 11:1 NKJV

Hope is the struggle of the soul, breaking loose from what is perishable and attesting her eternity.

Herman Melville

❧

Hope is faith holding out its hand in the dark.

Author Unknown

KEEPING WATCH

A Moment to Rest

When you see an officer in uniform on a street corner or a security guard at the shopping mall, do you get a sense of safety? Are you comforted simply by knowing someone is in charge and keeping watch in order to keep you protected?

In God's faithfulness lies eternal security.

Corrie ten Boom

In the early days of World War II, many people feared the enemy would attack North America. Home guards were created, and soon millions of volunteers, people who were ineligible for military service because of age or medical condition, became air-raid wardens. They wore official uniforms—white metal helmets and a whistle—and patrolled the streets during air-raid drills. They were well trained for fire and medical emergencies as well. Knowing that home guards were in place keeping watch for enemy planes or suspicious activity brought a sense of assurance to families during uncertain times.

Close your eyes and picture God as your personal security guard. You have a watchman who always has his eyes peeled for danger. He is keeping watch, maintaining constant surveillance in your life. He is capable of handling any crisis that may come from any direction. He never leaves you unguarded.

A Moment to Reflect

You are a hiding place for me; you preserve me from trouble; you surround me with shouts of deliverance.

Psalm 32:7 ESV

Because you belong to God, your security isn't based on something that is short-lived. He will never go away for a more important call. Because your confidence is in God, you have the solid assurance that he'll be at hand during every storm to protect and guide you. If you walk through darkness, he will be your constant escort. Trust him to be your defense. There are no chinks in God's armor, and his arsenal is more immense than can be imagined. God is your shield, and he can still the unrest in your heart.

You're never alone with Jesus,
He's always at your side,
Giving strength and wisdom
With you, he will abide.
To keep you safe from danger
The trials that come your way
You're never alone with Jesus
He's with you every day.

Colette Fedor

I shall not die, but I shall live, and recount the deeds of the LORD. . . . Open to me the gates of righteousness, that I may enter through them and give thanks to the LORD. This is the gate of the LORD; the righteous shall enter through it. I thank you that you have answered me and have become my salvation.

Psalm 118:17, 19–21 NRSV

A Moment to Refresh

The LORD is my light and my salvation;
Whom shall I fear?
The LORD is the defense of my life;
Whom shall I dread?

Psalm 27:1 NASB

Angels guard you
when you walk
with Me.
What better way
could you choose?

Frances J. Roberts

LORD, you have assigned me my portion and
my cup; you have made my lot secure.

Psalm 16:5 NIV

He will order his angels to
protect you wherever you go.

Psalm 91:11 NLT

Protect me, my
Lord, my boat is
so small, and your
ocean is so big.

Breton Fisherman's
Prayer

Don't be afraid of sudden disasters or storms
that strike those who are evil. You can be sure
that the LORD will protect you from harm.

Proverbs 3:25–26 CEV

Yea, though I walk through the valley of the
shadow of death, I will fear no evil;
For You are with me;
Your rod and Your staff, they comfort me.

Psalm 23:4 NKJV

NOURISHING MOMENTS

A Moment to Rest

Fresh bread baking in the oven, steak and onions sizzling on the grill, coffee brewing—every woman knows that food is more than just nourishment for the body. It's also a feast for the senses. Fix yourself a small snack right now. Make sure that whatever you prepare combines at least two ingredients. The menu can be as simple as a piece of toast with jelly or a cup of hot tea with lemon and honey.

The discovery of a new dish does more for the happiness of mankind than the discovery of a star.

Jean Anthelme
Brillat-Savarin

Taste each ingredient separately as you prepare your snack. Then sit down and enjoy the finished culinary combination. Resist the temptation to read the paper, chat on the phone, or even gaze out the window. Take a moment to savor every bite. Pay attention to the texture, the temperature, the aroma. Notice the unique taste you're experiencing. Consider how different the ingredients taste once they are combined.

Thank God for the wonderful experience he designed to accompany the simple act of being nourished. Praise him for the wide variety of flavors and textures he has provided to please your palate. From artichokes to zucchini, relish the smorgasbord God has set before you. Give thanks for every meal you can sit down and enjoy.

A Moment to Reflect

Oh, taste and see that the LORD is good;
Blessed is the man who trusts in Him!

Psalm 34:8 NKJV

In the Old Testament, God provided manna for the Israelites to eat when their food became scarce in the desert. It not only filled up their stomachs, but it also had a honeylike taste to please their palates. God has also shown the same care in providing for you. Not only has he made food for you to eat, but in addition, he has provided a wide variety of pleasing choices.

Before you begin your meal, bow your head for a moment, acknowledge God, and let him know you are genuinely grateful for what he has so generously provided—food that not only satisfies your hunger but also satisfies your spirit.

We may live without poetry, music and art;
We may live without conscience,
And live without heart;
We may live without friends;
We may live without books;
But civilized man cannot live without cooks.

Edward Robert Bulwer-Lytton

Eat your meals heartily, not worrying about what others say about you—you're eating to God's glory. . . . As a matter of fact, do everything that way, heartily and freely to God's glory.

1 Corinthians 10:31 MSG

A Moment to Refresh

Give us today our daily bread.

Matthew 6:11 HCSB

❧

I will bless you as long as I live; I will lift up my hands and call on your name. My soul is satisfied as with a rich feast, and my mouth praises you with joyful lips.

Psalm 63:4–5 NRSV

❧

Your promises are sweet to me, sweeter than honey in my mouth!

Psalm 119:103 NCV

❧

I, the LORD your God, [say,] "Open your mouth wide, and I will fill it with good things. I would satisfy you with wild honey from the rock."

Psalm 81:10, 16 NLT

❧

[Jesus said,] "I am the living bread that came down from heaven. If anyone eats of this bread, he will live forever."

John 6:51 ESV

One must ask children and birds how cherries and strawberries taste.

Johann Wolfgang von Goethe

❧

Know that even when you are in the kitchen, our Lord moves amidst the pots and pans.

Teresa of Avila

IF YOU WANT THE RAINBOW

A Moment to Rest

Sometimes things go wrong all day—your computer freezes up during an important project, you get a flat tire, the washing machine hose bursts. It is easy to lose perspective at times like these. Dolly Parton once said, "The way I see it, if you want the rainbow, you gotta put up with the rain." Some days it seems we see more rain than rainbow.

> *Every day, see how many things you can be thankful for. Say them over to yourself. Face the difficulties. They have to be dealt with. But, a positive, thankful psychology has written in it the power to make things good, better, best.*
>
> Norman Vincent Peale

Pause a moment to think of something you can give thanks for. Maybe it's a friend who sent you a card. Perhaps it's the stranger who returned money you dropped in the grocery line. Maybe it's the coupon you clipped for a discount on an oil change.

Remind yourself you have an abundance of things to be grateful for that enrich, brighten, and sweeten your life. All around you are the signs of God's love. Point them out to yourself and watch them multiply. The more you give thanks, the more reasons you'll find to be thankful.

Then tell others how thankful you are. Thank the store clerk for her efficiency, the bus driver for getting you there safely, the gardener for making your lawn beautiful. See how many hearts you can lift and smiles you can elicit.

A Moment to Reflect

You did it: you changed wild lament into whirling dance;
You ripped off my black mourning band and decked me
with wildflowers. I'm about to burst with song; I can't
keep quiet about you. GOD, my God,
I can't thank you enough.

Psalm 30:11–12 MSG

When you begin to guide your thoughts toward thankfulness, disappointments and unsatisfied hopes quietly fade away. As you give thanks for the little things in life, you will sense a feeling of well-being. As you allow yourself to dwell on the things for which you are grateful, you will sense your spirits rise as your daily burdens are lightened.

Direct your mind toward God's goodness and the many unexpected surprises that await you. Be assured that he is in control. Troubles no longer will seem insurmountable; problems no longer will loom so large.

I give thanks, God, for all
You have so lovingly done for me!
For each need comes Your faithfulness.
During suffering comes Your compassion.
On every journey comes Your closeness.
My deepest praise sings out
in a blended anthem with believers
all over the world—thanking You for
the abundant life found in Christ Jesus!

Charlotte Adelsperger

A Moment to Refresh

Enter into His gates with thanksgiving,
And into His courts with praise.
Be thankful to Him, and bless His name.
For the LORD is good; His mercy is everlasting,
And His truth endures to all generations.

Psalm 100:4–5 NKJV

Let them give thanks to the LORD for his
unfailing love and his wonderful deeds for men,
for he satisfies the thirsty and fills the
hungry with good things.

Psalm 107:8–9 NIV

Everything God made is good, and nothing
should be refused if it is accepted with thanks,
because it is made holy by what God
has said and by prayer.

1 Timothy 4:4–5 NCV

You received Christ Jesus, the Master; now live
him. You're deeply rooted in him. . . . You know
your way around the faith. . . . Let your living
spill over into thanksgiving.

Colossians 2:6–7 MSG

Cultivate a
thankful spirit!
It will be to you a
perpetual feast.

John R. MacDuff

Let us give thanks
for Someone
to thank.

Gerhard E. Frost

FAMILY FOCUS

A Moment to Rest

Energize yourself by taking a few minutes to relax and reflect on the family God has given you. Perhaps you can picture your sister's face as you played a childhood game, or you might remember your brother's face opening a longed-for birthday present. Focus on your parents' faces and the happy times you've spent with your mother and father. Remember the faces of people who touched your life and are now gone.

> *Loving relationships are a family's best protection against the challenges of the world.*
>
> Bernie Wiebe

Your family members are gifts from God meant to be treasured and appreciated here on earth. They love you, stand up for you, and fill your heart with unspeakable joy. Most of all they make you feel connected. They provide you with a sense of identity and a place to belong. Cherish the memory of times spent with grandparents and parents, aunts and uncles. Consider ways to pass down family traditions.

As you focus on the good times—laughs, hugs, unique family activities—thank God for making it all possible, for bringing you together and keeping you together through the good times and the not-so-good times. And give thanks for those people who seem like family, those special people placed in your life to bless you.

A Moment to Reflect

*May the LORD make you increase, both you and your
children. May you be blessed by the LORD,
the Maker of heaven and earth.*

Psalm 115:14–15 NIV

The concept of family is one of God's own making.
Throughout the pages of the Bible he consistently
demonstrates his commitment to the family unit and
the importance of family life. Just as we have family
here on earth, God also wants us to be a part of his
extended family and have an eternal family home. In
order to make it possible for us to become part of his
family, he gave his only Son to save us.

As you spend time thinking about your earthly family
and being grateful for all they mean to you, don't forget to thank God for inviting you into the greatest family of all—the family of God. What could be more
refreshing and comforting than knowing that you are
his own child and he has a home waiting for you?

*There's no vocabulary
For love within a family,
Love that's lived in
But not looked at,
Love within the light of which
All else is seen,
The love within which
All other love finds speech.
This love is silent.*

T. S. Eliot

People everywhere will remember and will turn
to the LORD. All the families of the
nations will worship him.

Psalm 22:27 NCV

❧

He gives the childless woman a family,
making her a happy mother.

Psalm 113:9 NLT

❧

Ascribe to the LORD, O families of the peoples,
ascribe to the LORD glory and strength!

Psalm 96:7 ESV

❧

[Cornelius] and all his family were devout and
God-fearing; he gave generously to those in
need and prayed to God regularly.

Acts 10:2 NIV

❧

I bow my knees before the Father, from whom
every family in heaven and on earth
derives its name.

Ephesians 3:14–15 NASB

❧

Every generation of those who serve you
will live in your presence.

Psalm 102:28 CEV

Other things may
change us, but we
start and end
with family.

Anthony Brandt

❧

Earthly fathers
and mothers, hus-
bands, wives, chil-
dren and earthly
friends, are all
"shadows."
But God is the
"substance."

Jonathan Edwards

SOOTHING WITH SONG

A Moment to Rest

Stop a moment and listen to a bird as it warbles and chirps. You'll hear the voice of nature, the sound of music in its purest form. On the fifth day of creation, God said, "Let the birds increase on the earth." Could it be that he wanted the world to have music from the

Next to theology, I give to music the highest place and honor. Music is the art of the prophets, the only art that can calm the agitation of the soul; it is one of the most magnificent and delightful presents God has given us.

Martin Luther

very start? Music and song have an incredible charm and magic. They can soothe your inner spirit and fill you with delight.

What kind of music do you enjoy? A classical piece, a traditional hymn? Maybe you like a lively country song, a good jazz ensemble, or today's more contemporary sounds. Perhaps lyrics or tunes sometimes float in your memory for days after hearing them because the music has touched you in a deep and profound way.

William Congreve's often misquoted verse actually reads, "Music hath charms to soothe the savage breast, to soften rocks, or bend a knotted oak." Music is one of God's greatest gifts to us, so surround yourself with the music you love. Let the music soothe you and fill you with delight. Relax as the music lifts and revives your spirit.

A Moment to Reflect

David told the leaders of the Levites to appoint their brothers as singers to play their lyres, harps, and cymbals and to sing happy songs.

1 Chronicles 15:16 NCV

Music was an important part of worship and celebration in biblical days. Singing soon became a way to express thankfulness to God. King David, a musician since boyhood, wrote many psalms and set them to music. He organized choirs to perform at the temple worship services.

Think of God as the great conductor, the ultimate musician. Music and worship fit naturally together. You can worship in your car as you pop in a CD of favorite hymns, plug in your favorite MP3 player and take a walk outdoors, or simply listen to one of nature's melodies as a bird sings outside your window. The next time you enjoy your favorite music, thank God for it. Ask him to speak to you through a song or a hymn or a bird's symphonic trilling.

And the night shall be filled with music,
And the cares that infest the day,
Shall fold their tents like the Arabs,
And as silently steal away.

Henry Wadsworth Longfellow

A Moment to Refresh

*Music is God's
best gift to man,
The only art
of heaven given
to earth,
The only art of
earth we take
to heaven.*

Letitia Elizabeth
Landon

❧

*Who among us
has not sought
peace in a song?*

Victor Hugo

*Shout joyfully to the LORD, all the earth;
Break forth and sing for joy and sing praises.
Sing praises to the LORD.*

Psalm 98:4–5 NASB

❧

*Sing praises to the LORD, O you his faithful
ones, and give thanks to his holy name.*

Psalm 30:4 NRSV

❧

*Sing praises to God and to his name!
Sing loud praises to him who rides the clouds.*

Psalm 68:4 NLT

❧

*The LORD is my strength and my song;
he has become my salvation. He is
my God, and I will praise him,
my father's God, and I will exalt him.*

Exodus 15:2 NIV

❧

*Be happy and shout to God who makes us
strong! . . . Sing as you play tambourines and
the lovely sounding stringed instruments.*

Psalm 81:1–2 CEV

CELEBRATE!

A Moment to Rest

Some celebrations take place in the quietest of moments simply to commemorate small victories. Take time for a small celebration right now. Find a comfortable spot—and bring along a candle.

Before you light the candle, choose the theme for your celebration. It could be as simple as the start of a brand-new day. Perhaps it's the completion of a project at work, the risk you took in confronting a friend, the gift of healing for a friend who was sick, or a milestone in your quest to become a woman of godly character.

> *All our life is a celebration for us; we are convinced, in fact, that God is always everywhere.*
>
> Clement of Alexandria

As you light your candle, give thanks for the event you are celebrating, for God's resources provided on your behalf, and for the people who helped to make it possible. Feel free to let your emotions flow—laugh, weep, sing, shout, and praise—until you've shown your gratitude.

Before you blow out your candle, consider how to carry the joy of the celebration with you throughout your day. Present someone with a rose to celebrate another day of friendship. Surprise your neighbors or office staff with a batch of cookies. Celebrate the victories you've been able to accomplish.

A Moment to Reflect

A time to cry and a time to laugh. A time to grieve and a time to dance. . . . There is nothing better than to be happy and enjoy ourselves as long as we can.

Ecclesiastes 3:4, 12 NLT

After God created the world, he took a day off to rest and celebrate what he had done. The start of each precious day presents a fresh opportunity for you. Today is filled with new beginnings. You will have a chance to make the most of these brand-new blocks of time. God has never created another twenty-four hours just like it. Use each one to the best of your ability.

Getting in the habit of celebrating the little things as well as the big things will help you become more aware of how priceless every day is, how extraordinary, and how praiseworthy. Reflect on God's example by looking around you and acknowledging what you have accomplished with his help. As God saw that "it was good," so you should celebrate and give thanks for all that is good in each day.

The soul of one who loves God
always swims in joy,
always keeps holiday,
and is always in a mood for singing.

John of the Cross

Be full of joy in the Lord always.
I will say again, be full of joy.

Philippians 4:4 NCV

Nehemiah said, "Go and enjoy choice food and
sweet drinks, and send some to those who
have nothing prepared. This day is
sacred to our Lord."

Nehemiah 8:10 NIV

✤

The whole assembly decided to celebrate the
feast another seven days, so they celebrated
the seven days with joy.

2 Chronicles 30:23 NASB

✤

God will rejoice over you as a bridegroom
rejoices over his bride.

Isaiah 62:5 NLT

✤

You have turned my sorrow into joyful dancing.

Psalm 30:11 CEV

✤

One generation shall laud your works to another, and shall declare your mighty acts. . . .
They shall celebrate the fame of your
abundant goodness, and shall sing
aloud of your righteousness.

Psalm 145:4, 7 NRSV

In seed time learn,
in harvest teach,
in winter enjoy.

William Blake

✤

The holiest of holi-
days are those
kept by ourselves
in silence and
apart; the secret
anniversaries of
the heart.

Henry Wadsworth
Longfellow

IN A CHILD'S EYES

A Moment to Rest

The wonderful thing about childhood enthusiasm is believing no obstacle is too great to overcome. There are no roadblocks, only challenges to meet and defeat. Everything is possible if you just want it, and nothing is impossible. Keep reaching for your goal until it is in your grasp. As we grow older, we often forget the sheer pleasure of pursuing a goal across unexplored territory. It is our loss when we do forget that feeling.

From her first breath, she captivates us and commands our attention. As she discovers the many wonders of life, her eager spirit and fresh perspective inspire us to appreciate the world anew through her eyes.

Arlene Benedict

The eagerness to venture beyond boundaries toward possibilities can be seen in a child's sparkling eyes. Now think back to the time when you were young and eager to explore the whole world through endless play. Remember when it seemed you could do everything and have fun doing it?

When was the last time you climbed on a swing at the park or rode a merry-go-round until you were dizzy? When was the last time you skipped stones or blew bubbles from a jar? When was the last time you tried to win a footrace, kicked a ball, or jumped rope? Look now for chances to experience a child's-eye view, and see the world and all its fresh and new possibilities.

A Moment to Reflect

We walk by faith, not by sight. . . . If anyone is in
Christ, he is a new creature; the old things passed
away; behold, new things have come.

2 Corinthians 5:7, 17 NASB

As a little girl, you were innocent and always hopeful, filled with simple faith. All you needed was a loving look and a gentle touch to feel secure and content. You knew faith and trust, which are second nature to a child.

Jesus said that everyone should have a childlike faith. Pray for that right now. Know that God will shelter you and provide all your needs. Your faith can be a wide-eyed, innocent faith that accepts and waits, a faith without question marks, a faith that accepts that understanding will come later.

To be a child . . . It is to believe in love, to believe in
loveliness, to believe in belief; it is to be so little that
the elves can reach to whisper in your ear; it is to
turn pumpkins into coaches and mice into horses,
lowness into loftiness and nothing into everything,
for each child has its fairy godmother in its soul.

Francis Thompson Shelly

"If you can do anything, have compassion on us and help
us." And Jesus said to him, "If you can! All things
are possible for one who believes."

Mark 9:22–23 ESV

A Moment to Refresh

Children have neither past nor future; and that which seldom happens to us, they rejoice in the present.

Jean de La Bruyère

❧

Children are God's apostles, day by day Sent forth to preach of love, and hope, and peace.

James Russell Lowell

Jesus had a child stand near him. He put his arm around the child and said, "When you welcome even a child because of me, you welcome me. And when you welcome me, you welcome the one who sent me."

Mark 9:36–37 CEV

❧

Some children were brought to Him so that He might lay His hands on them and pray; and the disciples rebuked them. But Jesus said, "Let the children alone, and do not hinder them from coming to Me; for the kingdom of heaven belongs to such as these."

Matthew 19:13–14 NASB

❧

[Jesus said,] "Whoever humbles himself like this child is the greatest in the kingdom of heaven."

Matthew 18:4 NIV

❧

Blessed are the pure in heart, for they shall see God. . . . Rejoice and be exceedingly glad, for great is your reward in heaven.

Matthew 5:8, 12 NKJV

POWER CHECKUP

The idea of a checkup is to forestall any potential problems. Take a few minutes to check up on your spiritual connection. Do a brief inventory of what keeps you connected to God. Do you pray? Study your Bible? Journal your thoughts and concerns? Read an inspirational bestseller? Reach out to others with God's love? All of these actions are good for boosting energy and for maintaining your spiritual resources.

> *We are the wire. God is the current. Our only power is to let the current pass through us.*
>
> Carlo Carretto

In any area where you feel there could be a future problem, figure out now how you can avoid it. Write down your solution. Make a list, if necessary. Choose one thing on your list that you can do right this minute. Then just do it. Pray, journal, pick up your Bible, or make that phone call. Afterward, reflect on how you feel more empowered as a woman and as a child of God by taking that one small step.

God wired everyone, including capable women like you, to work hand in hand with him. An eventual power outage is guaranteed if you try to do it all on your own. The only way to keep the power in your life is to keep the connection with the Source of all power.

A Moment to Reflect

Praise the LORD, because he alone is great. He is more wonderful than heaven and earth.

Psalm 148:13 NCV

One way to spiritually ground yourself is to get plugged into a local church. That means showing up on Sunday to hear someone speak—but it also means preparing your heart to learn from what you hear. It means being real with the people you meet. It means developing relationships and joining together by participating in prayer and praise. It means sharing your resources—your time, treasure, and talents. It may mean getting involved in Bible study, helping out in the nursery, or singing in the choir.

Whatever becoming actively involved in a church community may mean to you, it will help strengthen your connection to God as well as recharge your inner spirit.

The spacious firmament on high
With all the blue ethereal sky,
And spangled heavens, a shining frame,
Their great Original proclaim:
The unwearied sun, from day to day,
Does his Creator's power display,
And publishes to every land
The work of an almighty hand.

Joseph Addison

He has made the earth by His power,
He has established the world by His wisdom.

Jeremiah 10:12 NKJV

❧

The prayer of a person living right with God is
something powerful to be reckoned with.

James 5:16 MSG

❧

Praise God in his sanctuary. . . . Praise him
for his acts of power; praise him for
his surpassing greatness.

Psalm 150:1–2 NIV

❧

You will receive power when the
Holy Spirit has come upon you.

Acts 1:8 NASB

❧

I pray that Christ Jesus and the church will
forever bring praise to God. His power at
work in us can do far more than we dare
ask or imagine. Amen.

Ephesians 3:20–21 CEV

Confidence should
arise from
beneath, and
power descend
from above.

Emmanuel Joseph
Sieyés

❧

There is no limit
to the power of a
good woman.

Robert Hugh
Benson

A FRIEND INDEED

A Moment to Rest

Friends come and go, but some share special pieces of your past and warm up your world. Gail discovered this at her first class reunion when she saw her old gang, the true-blue friends who were more like sisters. They cheered at football games, decorated for proms, and huddled in sleeping bags, giggling over boys.

Friends in your life are like pillars on your porch. Sometimes they hold you up, and sometimes they lean on you. Sometimes it's just enough to know they're standing by.

Author Unknown

Catching up on each other's lives, they celebrated each other's jobs, loves, and dreams come true. And they cried—over illnesses, struggles, and disappointments. When the night was over, they knew they didn't want to let their friendship slip away again. Now they rent a cabin once a year for a long weekend, frolic like carefree teenagers, and share their deepest thoughts, hopes, and fears. They may not solve any problems, but they bolster each other up and leave refreshed.

Do you have an old friend from way back when? When you dared to be yourself, when you felt accepted and loved? Find out where she is now and then call or write her. Tell her how much she means to you, how you cherish the memories the two of you share. Set a date to get together with her, and then do it.

May my friends sing and shout for joy. May they always say, "Praise the greatness of the LORD, who loves to see his servants do well. I will tell of your goodness and will praise you every day."

Psalm 35:27–28 NCV

It has been said that a faithful friend is someone who believes in you and accepts you exactly the way you are, someone who speaks the painful truth with loving words, someone with whom you feel safe and at peace, someone who offers a warm hug when you face disappointment and a hearty applause with every success.

It has been said that a faithful friend is an image of God, that a faithful friend is someone who understands who you are, where you've been, everything you've gone through. God will wrap his arms around you through the arms of a good friend and through her remind you that he can always be reached.

We all need God's mercy,
We all need God's love.
We all need forgiveness
And grace from above.
We all need redemption,
We all need a Friend.
We all need a Savior
To have peace within.

Jan McIntosh

A Moment to Refresh

The fingers of God touch your life when you touch a friend.

Mary Dawn Hughes

❧

Girlfriends are forever friends when they're bound together with the love of God.

Janet Holm McHenry

Oil and perfume rejoice the heart; so does the sweetness of a friend's counsel that comes from the heart.

Proverbs 27:9 AMP

❧

[Jesus said,] "Greater love has no one than this, that he lay down his life for his friends. . . . I have called you friends, for everything that I learned from my Father I have made known to you. You did not choose me, but I chose you and appointed you to go and bear fruit—fruit that will last. . . . This is my command: Love each other."

John 15:13, 15–17 NIV

❧

Beloved, let us love one another, for love is from God, and whoever loves has been born of God and knows God.

1 John 4:7 ESV

❧

Jesus said, "For where two or three are gathered together in My name, I am there in the midst of them."

Matthew 18:20 NKJV

THE NOT-SO-IMPOSSIBLE DREAM

A Moment to Rest

Spiritual bifocals are essential to leading a visionary life. They help you focus clearly both close up (on what is happening now) and far away (on what is yet to happen). Put on a pair right now. Now close your eyes and dare to dream.

First, ground your dreams in reality. Use those imaginary bifocals to focus closely on where you are right now. Picture your daily routine. Ask yourself: What gives me energy? What wears me down? What would I like to change? What areas and abilities would I like to improve? What relationships would I like to make? What relationships would I like to see grow deeper?

> *Vision encompasses vast vistas outside the realm of the predictable, the safe, the expected.*
>
> Charles R. Swindoll

Last, change your focus to the future. Picture yourself in ten . . . twenty . . . forty years. What do you look like in your mind's eye? What dreams would you like to see come true before you leave this earth? How can you see God using the abilities he's given you more than he is now? Is there anything you can do now to better prepare for the future? Dream big. Dream bold.

Dream the impossible. With God, the impossible can happen.

A Moment to Reflect

*Delight yourself in the LORD and he will give you the
desires of your heart. Commit your way to the
LORD; trust in him and he will do this.*

Psalm 37:4–5 NIV

When you were little, you may have dreamed of
becoming a ballerina, an astronaut, or a rock-'n'-roll
singer. As you mature and grow closer to God, your
vision for the future may change. You may still long to
be a star, but most of all, you want to be the woman
God has created you to become—wherever that may
lead you. In God's eyes, who you are is of greater
importance than what you do.

Like any father, God loves to give his children what
they long for, although his vision for your life may differ from your own. He knows the desires of your heart,
your hopes, and dreams. He hears all your prayers and
will help you to be your best as he fulfills your needs.

*Vision that looks inward becomes duty.
Vision that looks outward becomes aspiration.
Vision that looks upward becomes faith.*

Author Unknown

*If people can't see what God is doing,
they stumble all over themselves;
But when they attend to what he reveals,
they are most blessed. . . .
The fear of human opinion disables;
trusting in GOD protects you from that.*

Proverbs 29:18, 25 MSG

May he grant your heart's desire and
fulfill all your plans.

Psalm 20:4 NLT

❧

You open your hand
And satisfy the desire of every living thing.
The LORD is righteous in all his ways
And kind in all His deeds.

Psalm 145:16–17 NASB

❧

Jesus said, "All things are possible with God."

Mark 10:27 NASB

❧

"No eye has seen, no ear has heard, and no
mind has imagined what God has prepared for
those who love him." . . . We have received God's
Spirit (not the world's spirit), so we can know
the wonderful things God has freely given us.

1 Corinthians 2:9, 12 NLT

❧

One night the Lord said to Paul in a vision,
"Do not be afraid, but speak and do not be
silent; for I am with you."

Acts 18:9–10 NRSV

Vision is the art of
seeing things
invisible.

Jonathan Swift

❧

O Lord, this is our
desire, to walk
along the path of
life that you have
appointed us, in
steadfastness of
faith, in lowliness
of heart, in gentle-
ness of love.

Maria Hare

REST STOPS

A Moment to Rest

Imagine a dusty attic with a tiny window. There is an old dresser that held all your baby things, sleepers, and sweaters, all folded neatly. Breathe deeply. Can you smell the sweet talcum powder? In the corner, see the old trunk with tarnished metal corners and leather straps? Look inside. It's full of old feathery hats, high-heeled shoes, costume jewelry, and glittery gowns. Can you think of yourself all dressed up like a princess, playing make-believe, hosting a tea party for your favorite dolls?

> *Memory is the cabinet of imagination, the treasury of reason, the registry of conscience, and the council chamber of thought.*

As you enjoy this moment, try to remember a specific pleasure from your past. Perhaps it was the first day you rode the bicycle with the training wheels removed, finding a seashell on the beach, or when you read your first love letter. Perhaps it was graduation, a wonderful Christmas, a special vacation.

Nothing is more soothing than thinking about cherished memories that take you back to a precious time. Memories like these are only meant to be rest stops along the way, places to drink in the wonder of days gone by, not to wish them back, but to relish them as part of you—who you were and who you will become.

A Moment to Reflect

God can do anything, you know — far more than you
could ever imagine. . . . He does it not by pushing
us around but by working within us, his
Spirit deeply and gently within us.

Ephesians 3:20 MSG

Sometimes the attic may seem a bit musty, the relics covered in dust, the ink faded on cherished letters. Let God explore with you. Let him share the treasures in your heart. Stop and rest as he fills your mind with pleasant memories and good feelings as you look around your life.

When God jogs your mind about the past, it won't be about regrets or wounds you'd rather forget. He'll prompt you with warm thoughts that will affirm who you are and who you were meant to be, thoughts that refresh, renew, and never fail to bring a smile.

God can paint rich hues on the misty memories of my past.
He can shine a guiding ray on my choices for the future.
But God's love reigns best when he, in nearness,
holds this very moment in his hands.

Charlotte Adelsperger

❧

I remember the days of old. I ponder all your great works. I
think about what you have done. I reach out for you. I
thirst for you as parched land thirsts for rain.

Psalm 143:5–6 NLT

A Moment to Refresh

I have a room where into no one enters, save I myself alone. There sits a blessed memory on a throne. There, my life centers.

Christina Rossetti

❧

We must always have old memories and young hopes.

Arsene Houssaye

I will remember the deeds of the LORD; yes, I will remember your wonders of old. I will ponder all your work, and meditate on your mighty deeds.

Psalm 77:11–12 ESV

❧

I will always remind you about these things, even though you know them and are established in the truth you have. I consider it right . . . to wake you up with a reminder.

2 Peter 1:12–13 HCSB

❧

Give thanks to the LORD, call on his name, make known his deeds among the peoples. Sing to him, sing praises to him, tell of all his wonderful works.

1 Chronicles 16:8–9 NRSV

❧

The LORD appeared to us in the past, saying: "I have loved you with an everlasting love; I have drawn you with loving-kindness. I will build you up again and you will be rebuilt."

Jeremiah 31:3–4 NIV

Spirit Shape-Up

A Moment to Rest

When trying to gain physical strength, you go to the gym. When trying to strengthen your inner spirit, you go to God. Do it now. Ask him to reveal your areas of strength and weakness. Thank him for any natural strengths. Ask for insight to use your strengths in a way that will cause others to praise him.

Take a close, honest look at your weaknesses. This is the first step in creating a personal workout program to strengthen your character as well as your spirit. As any personal trainer will tell you, building strength doesn't happen overnight. It takes repeated exercise focused on specific areas. Choose one specific area now. Then choose an exercise that will turn this flabby feature into pure muscle.

> *One drop of God's strength is worth more than all the world.*
>
> Dwight L. Moody

If fear keeps you from moving forward in your life, find a Scripture that reminds you of God's protection. Memorize that verse and repeat it to yourself every time the butterflies in your stomach take flight. If you're struggling with a quick temper, practice holding your tongue. Whenever you get irritated pause and think before speaking rashly. Getting yourself in shape physically and mentally takes practice, patience, and perseverance. The benefits last a lifetime.

A Moment to Reflect

I can do all things through Him who strengthens me. . . .
My God will supply all your needs
according to His riches in glory in Christ Jesus.

Philippians 4:13, 19 NASB

As any woman who works out regularly at the gym can testify, having a workout partner can keep you going when you'd rather stop and throw in the towel. The same is true for your spiritual workout. Ask a close friend to be an accountability partner. Choose someone you trust implicitly and respect spiritually. Then dare to bare your weaknesses.

Give your friend permission to ask you how your exercise program is progressing. Ask her to share any additional areas of weakness she sees. Be vulnerable and humble enough to accept both criticism and praise. Praying together will strengthen both of you.

"As the day thy strength shall be!"
This should be enough for thee;
He who knows thy frame will spare
Burdens more than thou canst bear.
When thy days are veiled in night,
Christ shall give thee heavenly light;
Seem they wearisome and long,
Yet in Him thou shalt be strong.

Frances Ridley Havergal

God is my strong fortress;
he has made my way safe.

2 Samuel 22:33 NLT

❦

I love you, LORD; my strength.

Psalm 18:1 HCSB

❦

The LORD is my strength and my might,
and he has become my salvation.

Exodus 15:2 NRSV

❦

Don't be sad, because the joy of the
LORD will make you strong.

Nehemiah 8:10 NCV

❦

I take limitations in stride, and with good
cheer, these limitations that cut me down to
size —abuse, accidents, opposition, bad breaks.
I just let Christ take over! And so the
weaker I get, the stronger I become.

2 Corinthians 12:10 MSG

❦

Good people will prosper like palm trees, and
they will grow strong like the cedars of
Lebanon. They will take root in your house,
LORD God, and they will do well.

Psalm 92:12–13 CEV

We must always
change, renew,
rejuvenate
ourselves; other-
wise we harden.

Johann Wolfgang
von Goethe

❦

Faith is kept alive
in us, and gathers
strength, more
from practice than
from speculations.

Joseph Addison

DAILY LAUGHTER

A Moment to Rest

Do you laugh regularly? Laughter helps decrease the mood-altering hormones that play havoc with your attitude. Laughing can lower your blood pressure, expand the chest, and clear out the brain. Anything that reduces stress and makes you feel better can be one of the best and least expensive medicines.

> *Mirth is God's medicine. Everybody ought to bathe in it. Grim care, moroseness, anxiety—all this rust of life ought to be scoured off by the oil of mirth.*
>
> Henry Ward Beecher

A gentle chuckle to a hearty giggle to fall-out-of-your-chair laughter can be uplifting for the spirit. It is a shock absorber that eases the blows of life. While it won't erase the problem, it can sure make things more bearable, especially if shared with a friend.

Resolve to incorporate humor into your life. Create a humor first-aid kit—your own survival gear for stressful times. Fill it with things that tickle your funny bone—jokes, quotes, wind-up toys, witty cards, comedy DVDs, funny cartoons, crazy hats, rubber noses, old photos that make you smile, a list of amusing Web sites. Schedule a time each week to get out your kit and spend time laughing.

Humor is contagious. Make sure to pass it on. Call a friend to share a joke or e-mail one of your favorite stories. Send an amusing greeting card to someone who needs a good hearty chuckle today.

A Moment to Reflect

There's no way that God will reject a good person. . . .
God will let you laugh again; you'll raise
the roof with shouts of joy.

Job 8:20–21 MSG

Laughter is the most beneficial therapy God has given for the ills that attack your spirit. God wants you to laugh often. It's a sweet sound to his ears. When you find time to laugh at something every day you learn that if you can laugh at it, you can live with it.

Martin Luther said, "If you're not allowed to laugh in heaven, I don't want to go there." Certainly, laughter will be magnified in heaven, but it's here now, so indulge often. Joy, creativity, fun—these are God's creations, fringe benefits with which he has blessed us.

You and I were created for joy, and if we miss it, we miss the
reason for our existence. . . . If our joy is honest joy, it must
somehow be congruous with human tragedy. This is the test
of joy's integrity; is it compatible with pain? Only the
heart that hurts has a right to joy.

Lewis B. Smedes

❦

Sarah said, "God has brought me laughter, and everyone
who hears about this will laugh with me."

Genesis 21:6 NIV

A Moment to Refresh

She is clothed with strength and dignity, and she laughs with no fear of the future.

Proverbs 31:25 NLT

❧

A glad heart makes a cheerful countenance, but by sorrow of heart the spirit is broken.

Proverbs 15:13 NRSV

❧

Laughter is a tranquilizer with no side effects.

Arnold H. Glasgow

❧

The light of the eyes rejoices the heart, and good news refreshes the bones.

Proverbs 15:30 ESV

❧

When the righteous see God in action they'll laugh, they'll sing, they'll laugh and sing for joy.

Psalm 68:3 MSG

❧

A good laugh heals a lot of hurts.

Madeleine L'Engle

He will yet fill your mouth with laughter and your lips with shouts of joy.

Job 8:21 NLT

❧

I will celebrate and be joyful because you, LORD, have saved me.

Psalm 35:9 CEV

WORDS OF LOVE

A Moment to Rest

Writing a letter is a wonderful way to express your love and concern for another person. The recipient may be someone who lives around the block or around the world. She may be a longtime friend or a person who has blessed your life.

Take out a sheet of paper, an informal note card, or—if you have a lot to say or your handwriting is difficult to read—sit down at your computer. If you choose to type instead of hand-write your letter, be sure to send it via regular mail rather than e-mail. You want to bless your friend with some-thing she can hold in her hands and reread when her heart needs a hug.

> *More than kisses, letters mingle souls; for thus friends absent speak.*
>
> John Donne

Take a moment to pray for the per-son you are about to write to. Then let your loving message flow. Emphasize the things you love about your friend. Enjoy the feelings of caring as you choose words of encouragement and support.

Don't rush as you write. Let your sincerity and friend-ship dictate every line. When you are finished, seal your letter with a prayer for your friend. Send your let-ter on its way and thank God for this relationship.

A Moment to Reflect

Friends love through all kinds of weather.

Proverbs 17:17 MSG

As Thomas Hughes once wrote, "Blessed are they who have the gift of making friends, for it is one of God's best gifts. It involves many things, but above all, the power of going out of one's self, and appreciating whatever is noble and loving in another."

Expressing how much you care for and appreciate someone by putting your feelings on paper is an act of love that nourishes you as much as it does the recipient. God performed this same act of love with his own love letter, the Bible. Much of the New Testament was written as letters to friends and churches, as God inspired each author. The word *epistle*, in fact, means "personal, handwritten correspondence."

So as you read the Bible, think of it as God's personal note written specifically for you. Why do you think God included what he did for you to read? What kind of response do you think his love letter is asking for? Be sure and thank him for his letter to you.

With fond affection true,
I write these lines for you;
By this token you may see,
I still remember thee.

Mary F. Traver

*Pleasant words are like a honeycomb, sweetness
to the soul and health to the body.*

Proverbs 16:24 NRSV

❦

*I have many things to write to you, but I do
not want to use paper and ink. Instead,
I hope to come to you and talk face
to face so we can be full of joy.*

2 John 1:12 NCV

❦

*I have written to you briefly, exhorting and tes-
tifying that this is the true grace of God.*

1 Peter 5:12 NASB

❦

*I give thanks to my God for you always
when I mention you in my prayers.*

Philemon 1:4 AMP

❦

*Worry weighs us down; a cheerful
word picks us up.*

Proverbs 12:25 MSG

❦

*The other believers here have asked me
to greet you for them. Greet each other
in Christian love. . . . My love to all
of you in Christ Jesus.*

1 Corinthians 16:20, 24 NLT

*When you receive
a letter from a
friend, you should
not hesitate to
embrace it as
a friend.*

Isidore of Seville

❦

*No distance of
place or lapse of
time can lessen
the friendship of
those who are
thoroughly
persuaded of
each other's
worth.*

Robert Southey

PRECIOUS TREASURE

A Moment to Rest

*L*ook around your home. What are the things you most treasure? Which things do you display with great care? What items would you want to protect if your house were burning? Think back to the last time you visited a museum.

> *The human soul is God's treasury, out of which he coins unspeakable riches. Thoughts and feelings, desires and yearnings, faith and hope — these are the most precious things that God finds in us.*
>
> Henry Ward Beecher

Museums are full of an assortment of rare books, precious one-of-a-kind documents, relics from past centuries, and treasures of ancient civilizations that are considered important and worth saving.

Imagine the people filing past many of these fragile objects, some enclosed in glass. You hear a respectful hush in the room, a sense of awe at the artifacts in view, a realization that these things are one of a kind and beyond monetary value. You leave knowing that you've been privileged to see the pieces of history preserved in these priceless treasures. You are grateful that these items are being preserved for generations to come.

Whenever you find your self-esteem wilting, envision this scene, and remember that you, too, are priceless—to God. He will go to great lengths to preserve and sustain you. You are his treasure—the best of his collection—and you are of immeasurable value to him.

A Moment to Reflect

The LORD God is like a sun and shield; the LORD gives us
kindness and honor. He does not hold back anything good
from those whose lives are innocent. . . . Happy are the
people who trust you!

Psalm 84:11–12 NCV

If you consider yourself to be one of God's treasures,
you can comprehend more of his depth and richness.
The more you understand how much you are worth to
God, the more cherished and accepted you will feel.
What a revelation! Regardless of your shortcomings,
the highest price imaginable was paid for you on the
cross in Jesus' sacrificing love.

You have a God who knows you thoroughly and who
values every facet of you, who knows how to bring out
your very best. Allow him access to your life. Let him
show you off to all the world, so that others will see his
goodness reflected through you.

God is God. Because He is God, He is worthy of my trust
and obedience. I will find rest nowhere but in His holy will,
a will that is unspeakably beyond my largest
notions of what He is up to.

Elisabeth Elliot

God has reaffirmed that you are dearly held treasure just as
he promised, a people entrusted with keeping his command-
ments, a people set high above all other nations.

Deuteronomy 26:18–19 MSG

A Moment to Refresh

God does not love us because we are valuable. We are valuable because God loves us.

Archbishop
Fulton J. Sheen

❦

You are God's dearly beloved and the object of His affection. The apple of His eye. Heir to His kingdom. He planned the redemption He makes real in you every day. When you respond by living your life with meaning, you reveal your commitment to the covenant between you and Him.

Kari West

God will be the sure foundation for your times, a rich store of salvation and wisdom and knowledge; the fear of the LORD is the key to this treasure.

Isaiah 33:6 NIV

❦

*Keep me as the apple of the eye;
Hide me in the shadow of Your wings.*

Psalm 17:8 NASB

❦

*LORD, You are the portion of
my inheritance and my cup;
You maintain my lot.
The lines have fallen to me in
pleasant places;
Yes, I have a good inheritance.*

Psalm 16:5–6 NKJV

❦

God, who said, "Let there be light in the darkness," has made this light shine in our hearts so we could know the glory of God that is seen in the face of Jesus Christ. We now have this light shining in our hearts, but we ourselves are like fragile clay jars containing this great treasure.

2 Corinthians 4:6–7 NLT

THE BEST OF FRIENDS

A Moment to Rest

A close encounter of the furry kind can be a great boost to your spirit. Think back to when you were a little child and recall the animals that were part of your life. Perhaps it was a personal pet, the pooch next door, or the lion at the zoo. What was it about that critter that made you smile? What did it do, look like, or feel like that warmed your heart? Which of its unique characteristics intrigued you, comforted you, or amused you?

If you have the privilege of sharing your home with a pet, take a break right now and spend some quality time. Take your pet in your arms (unless it's a goldfish), and hold it close. Experience how relaxing its rhythmic breathing or purring can be. Stroke its fur or fluff its feathers. How does your pet let you know it loves you? Tell your pet, and God, what you enjoy most about it.

All animals except man know that the principal business of life is to enjoy it.

Samuel Butler

Then treat your pet to some playtime, a walk, or a favorite treat. Chances are you will both come away feeling refreshed and invigorated. Connecting with one of God's creatures can be relaxing and rewarding, a unique balm to soothe you.

A Moment to Reflect

*GOD doesn't come and go. God lasts. He's Creator of all
you can see or imagine. He doesn't get tired out, doesn't
pause to catch his breath. And he knows everything, inside
and out. He energizes those who get tired, gives fresh
strength to dropouts. . . . But those who wait upon GOD get
fresh strength. They spread their wings and soar like eagles,
They run and don't get tired, they walk and don't lag behind.*

Isaiah 40:28–31 MSG

When God created animals, he put them under the
care of humans. While it's true he created them to
assist the human race, the sheer magnitude and mag-
nificence of the animal kingdom make it reasonable to
think that perhaps he created them for man's enjoy-
ment, as well.

Even the least enthusiastic animal lover can easily see
and appreciate what God has created in the animal kingdom. The diversity and details are incredible examples
of God's handiwork. God created every creature with
care and proclaimed it "good." So be sure to thank him
for each friend that passes through your life.

*He prayeth best, who loveth best
All things both great and small;
For the dear God who loveth us,
He made and loveth all.*

Samuel Taylor Coleridge

God said, "I command the earth to give life to
all kinds of tame animals, wild animals,
and reptiles." . . . God made every one of
them. . . . And it was good.

Genesis 1:24–25 CEV

❧

Your righteousness is like the mighty mountains, your justice like the ocean depths. You
care for people and animals alike, O LORD.

Psalm 36:6 NLT

❧

He provides the animals with their food, and
the young ravens, what they cry for.

Psalm 147:9 HCSB

❧

He will feed his flock like a shepherd; he will
gather the lambs in his arms, and carry them
in his bosom, and gently lead the mother sheep.

Isaiah 40:11 NRSV

❧

I know and am acquainted with all the birds
of the mountains, and the wild animals
of the field are Mine.

Psalm 50:11 AMP

I would give noth-
ing for that man's
religion whose
very dog and cat
are not the
better for it!

Rowland Hill

❧

Every single
creature is full
of God and is a
book about God.

Meister Eckhart

THE GIFT OF TODAY

A Moment to Rest

Try getting up before the sun rises. Find a silent place to see the dawn emerge. The first rays of light streaking across the sky seem to write on the horizon, *Today is a gift to you.* As you watch for that soaring burst of sun, let the serene beauty of that simple moment be stored in your mind to lift your spirit throughout the day.

Each day comes bearing gifts, Untie the ribbons.

Ann Ruth
Schabacker

The sun has been called the "eye of heaven," and its rising each day proclaims the glory of creation and symbolizes new life. Each time the sun peeks above the horizon, it brings a fresh promise—the gift of another day. Greet each day by beginning it well as you enjoy a quiet moment of renewal.

Develop your own routine for getting up in the morning—your personally designed "order of the day." Perhaps you like to wake up a little early, brew a special cup of tea or coffee, and, before it gets hectic, spend a few silent moments in anticipation of what this day might bring.

Seek the quiet comfort of your heart being renewed again with the miracle of a brand-new day. Give thanks for the gift of today.

A Moment to Reflect

I call to God; GOD will help me. At dusk, dawn, and noon
I sigh deep sighs — he hears, he rescues.

Psalm 55:16–17 MSG

Today God has given you twenty-four hours, a block of time carved specifically for you. Nobody else will have a day like yours. You will have a few frustrations, but you will also have enriching joys, hopes, and invitations that you won't want to miss.

God is merciful to lift the curtain on each day with a new dawn. With it comes inspiration and renewed strength. Be encouraged this day with the time God has given you. Let him show you the true value of these moments and how to enjoy them. Happiness can be yours today. Make the most of each waking hour. Be sure and pause during each twenty-four hours you're given to thank God for each moment he has granted you.

There is sunshine in my soul today,
More glorious and bright
Than glows in any earthly sky,
For Jesus is my Light.
There is gladness in my soul today,
And hope and praise and love,
For blessings which He gives me now,
For joys "laid up" above.

Eliza E. Hewitt

A Moment to Refresh

Yesterday is a canceled check, and tomorrow is a promissory note. But today is cash, ready for us to spend in living.

Barbara Johnson

❧

Normal day, let me be aware of the treasure you are. Let me learn from you, love you, savor you, bless you before I depart. Let me not pass by you in quest of some rare and perfect tomorrow. Let me hold you while I may for it will not always be so.

Mary Jean Irion

The heavens are telling the glory of God; and the firmament proclaims his handiwork.

Psalm 19:1 NRSV

❧

Let the morning bring me word of your unfailing love, for I have put my trust in you. Show me the way I should go, for to you I lift up my soul.

Psalm 143:8 NIV

❧

Listen to my voice in the morning, LORD. Each morning I bring my requests to you and wait expectantly.

Psalm 5:3 NLT

❧

Nothing on earth is more beautiful than the morning sun. Even if you live to a ripe old age, you should try to enjoy each day, because darkness will come and will last a long time.

Ecclesiastes 11:7–8 CEV

❧

The path of the righteous is like the light of dawn, which shines brighter and brighter until full day.

Proverbs 4:18 ESV

DEEP ROOTS

A Moment to Rest

A simple seed is a storehouse for miracles. Watch the daily ongoing wonder of creation by planting a packet of seeds. Choose something that's hardy and fast growing, such as marigolds, sweet peas, or beans. Read the directions on the package and then prepare to dig in and get dirt under your fingernails.

As you get ready to plant the seeds in your yard or in a window box, enjoy the smell of the earth. Imagine what the mature plant will look like. Compare that image to the tiny seed in your hand. Does the seed give any clue as to the miracle that lies ahead? After the seeds are planted, sit down and take at least five minutes to think about the growth process.

> *One is nearer God's heart in a garden than anywhere else on earth.*
>
> Dorothy Frances Gurney

Compare your life to the seeds you've just planted. What stage of growth is it in? Is your faith in God still in the freshly planted seed stage? Are there a few fragile green shoots peeking up from the soil? Do your roots go down deep, strengthened by both the sun and storms of life? Take time to ask God to help care for the seed of faith he's planted in you.

A Moment to Reflect

*GOD planted a garden in Eden, in the east. He put the
Man he had just made in it. GOD made all kinds of trees
grow from the ground, trees
beautiful to look at and good to eat.*

Genesis 2:8–9 MSG

Growth and change take time. Whether you are waiting
for a plant to sprout in your garden or a seed of faith
to blossom within you, maturity can be a slow process.
And waiting for that metamorphosis—the first
marigold bud or a trust in God that stands fast during
hard times—takes patience. You have all you need
when you rely on God. He will supply the patience and
the growth.

Be patient with yourself and with others as you wait for
growth to happen. Just like watching newly planted
seeds, growth isn't always evident to the eye. Many
things happen beneath the surface. The roots of the
seed often grow deep before the plant emerges. God
knows just the season and timetable needed to make
each plant or person flourish and grow into full
maturity.

*We plough the fields, and scatter
The good seed on the land,
But it is fed and water'd
By God's Almighty Hand.*

Ancient Hymn

God said, "I will send you rain in its season,
and the ground will yield its crops and the
trees of the field their fruit."

Leviticus 26:4 NIV

❦

Paul wrote: "I planted, Apollos watered, but
God gave the growth. So neither the one who
plants nor the one who waters is anything, but
only God who gives the growth."

1 Corinthians 3:6–7 NRSV

❦

God said, "Behold, I have given you every plant
yielding seed that is on the surface of all the
earth, and every tree which has fruit yielding
seed; it shall be food for you.

Genesis 1:29 NASB

❦

God will bless you in all your produce and in
all the work of your hands, so that you
will be altogether joyful.

Deuteronomy 16:15 ESV

*It is always
springtime in the
heart that
loves God.*

Jean-Baptiste
Marie Vianney

❦

*He who makes a
garden works
hand in hand
with God.*

Douglas Malloch

INNER LIGHT

A Moment to Rest

How often have you seen a striking painting, heard a song that moved you, or read a thought-provoking book, and wondered what inspired the creator to produce such a beautiful work? There is always some special spark that makes each such creation unique, and it is the skill of the artist who translates that spark into something inspirational and illuminating. The best of these creations seem to contain an inner light that brings our own lives into clearer focus.

> *A musician must make music, an artist must paint, a poet must write if he is ultimately to be at peace with himself. What one can be, one must be.*
>
> Abraham Maslow

In the very same way, each of us is a unique and special work of art created by God. He has given us each an inner fire. We can make the most of his gift by tending the flame and making our light shine.

Think of a piece of art you admire, and pretend you are the artist at the moment of inspiration. You are about to paint a masterpiece that will bring joy and comfort to many. That's the way God designed you. You are an original, a unique portrait, unlike any other piece of art that God has ever made or will ever make again. God will fill you with joy and an inner light that can be used to comfort many.

A Moment to Reflect

*The LORD is good to everyone; he is
merciful to all he has made.*

Psalm 145:9 NCV

The Bible says God created you, was pleased to make
you his own, and summons you by name. Take a
moment to dwell on the thought that you are an original, signed by the Master's own hand.

Before you were born he sketched a design of undeter-
mined value—you. You are the only one just like you.
You are number one; there is no number two or number
three. You are so much more than a limited edition—
you are an exclusive edition. Your inner character and
your special personality are evidence that you are truly
one of a kind.

*We master fear through faith—faith in the worthwhileness
of life and the trustworthiness of God; faith in the meaning
of our pain and our striving, and confidence that God will not
cast us aside but will use each one of us as a piece of
priceless mosaic in the design of his universe.*

Joshua Loth Liebman

*This is what the LORD says—he who created you . . . he who
formed you . . . "Fear not, for I have redeemed you; I have
summoned you by name; you are mine. . . .
Do not be afraid, for I am with you."*

Isaiah 43:1, 5 NIV

A Moment to Refresh

*Man is heaven's
masterpiece.*

Francis Quarles

⊗

*You aren't an
accident. You
weren't mass-pro-
duced. You aren't
an assembly-line
product. You were
deliberately
planned, specifi-
cally gifted, and
lovingly positioned
on this earth by
the Master
Craftsman.*

Max Lucado

*There's no one like her on earth, never has been,
never will be. She's a woman beyond compare.
My dove is perfection,
Pure and innocent as the day she was born.*

Song of Solomon 6:8–9 MSG

⊗

*Your new day is dawning. The glory of the
LORD shines brightly on you.*

Isaiah 60:1 CEV

⊗

*You are a chosen generation, a royal priesthood,
a holy nation, His own special people, that you
may proclaim the praises of Him who called
you out of darkness into His marvelous light.*

1 Peter 2:9 NKJV

⊗

*We are God's masterpiece. He has created us
anew in Christ Jesus, so that we can do the
good things he planned for us long ago.*

Ephesians 2:10 NLT

⊗

*Look at how great a love the Father has given
us, that we should be called God's children.
And we are!*

1 John 3:1 HCSB

SOOTHE YOURSELF

A Moment to Rest

Do you start running from the moment your alarm sounds and you roll out of bed in the morning—running car pools, running to the office, running to grab some lunch, running errands, and in the process, running yourself ragged? Think how good it would feel to slow yourself down to a comfortable walk.

So take five. Whether it's five minutes, five blocks, or five miles, get out your most comfortable pair of athletic shoes. When you put them on, use that action as a reminder to invite God to join you. As you get under way, breathe deeply and slowly. Focus on your heart beating, your lungs filling with air, and the muscles in your legs contracting. Thank God for the wonder of being a woman.

> *Thoughts come clearly while one walks.*
>
> Thomas Mann

As you begin to hit your stride, listen to the sounds around you—the birds in the trees, the laughter of children, a carillon ringing out the hour, the excited yips of dogs chasing each other. Notice the details— the warm breeze on your face, the flower growing in the crack of the sidewalk, the scent of bread as you pass a bakery. Let every step you take soothe you.

A Moment to Reflect

*We can make our plans, but the LORD
determines our steps.*

Proverbs 16:9 NLT

God wants to walk with you through your daily life just
as he walks with you on the sidewalk in front of your
house, on a tree-lined walking trail, or on an old dirt
road. He wants to walk with you through the good times
and the difficult times, on rainy days and sunny days.
God is kind and gentle. He's waiting for you to ask him
to come along with you.

We know that God promises to protect us when we walk
with him. We will be safe when we walk through life
sharing each step with the One who created it all. Open
your heart, ask him to come in and walk with you. You'll
be glad you did. If you follow in his footsteps and let
him guide you, you'll never walk alone again.

*Walk quietly —
And know that He is God.
When the dawn on winged steed comes riding high,
To blazon painted banners on the morning sky,
When evening shadows lie against the hill —
In the hush of twilight, when the world is still.
Walk quietly.*

Author Unknown

❧

*Early the next morning, while it was still dark, Jesus woke and
left the house. He went to a lonely place, where he prayed.*

Mark 1:35 NCV

[*Moses said:*] *"These commandments that I give you today are to be upon your hearts. Impress them on your children. Talk about them when you sit at home and when you walk along the road, when you lie down and when you get up."*

Deuteronomy 6:6–7 NIV

❧

The LORD requires of you: Only to act justly, to love faithfulness, and to walk humbly with your God.

Micah 6:8 HCSB

❧

Your ears will hear a word behind you, "This is the way, walk in it."

Isaiah 30:21 NASB

❧

Late in the afternoon . . . the man and woman heard the LORD God walking in the garden.

Genesis 3:8 CEV

❧

I will walk among you, and will be your God, and you shall be my people.

Leviticus 26:12 NRSV

God passes through the thicket of the world, and wherever his glance falls he turns all things to beauty.

John of Avila

❧

Climb the mountains and get their good tidings. Nature's peace will flow into you as sunshine flows into trees. The winds blow their freshness into you, and the storms their energy, while cares will drop off like falling leaves.

John Muir

ENJOY THE ORDINARY

A Moment to Rest

The world is impatient and fast changing, and progress is relentless. Technology is advancing at the speed of light. Nothing stays ordinary for long, so take a look around you now. Lean back on your personal observation deck and view the commonplace in your life.

Notice the run-of-the-mill things in your world, those plain, everyday occurrences that are so easy to neglect.

I find each day too short for all the thoughts I want to think, all the walks I want to take, all the books I want to read, and all the friends I want to see. The longer I live the more my mind dwells on the beauty and the wonder of the world.

John Burroughs

Look up at fleecy clouds moving across the sky. Examine the bud of a flower waiting to bloom. Listen to birds chirping and watch squirrels chasing each other around a tree. Revel in the dawning wonder on a baby's face and the laughter of the children as they board the school bus. See the kindness in a loved one's eyes, the determination on the face of a mountain biker straining to make the hill. Enjoy the smell of coffee brewing, the sound of a friendly, familiar voice when you answer the phone.

See the beauty in the ordinary. Slow down and inhale the fragrance of the ordinary, the everyday things that sit along life's way. It's as easy as looking out a window or taking a walk. Remind yourself often to stop and smell the flowers.

A Moment to Reflect

When they saw the courage of Peter and John and realized that they were unschooled, ordinary men, they were astonished and they took note that these men had been with Jesus.

Acts 4:13 NIV

As you enjoy the ordinary, songs will flow from your heart. As you delight in a rose growing in your neighbor's garden or a bird warbling on the telephone wire, you will take delight in observing the extraordinary ordinary.

God reveals his presence in the familiar—the leafy trees, the shadows cast, the trampled path. God reveals his presence in the beat of your heart and the breath you take. You have access to God's presence anywhere, anytime. The more you delight in the routine, you will discover yourself more satisfied, more grateful, and more in touch with God.

Have you ever realized that you can give things to God that are of value to Him? Or are you just sitting around daydreaming about the greatness of His redemption, while neglecting all the things you could be doing for Him? I'm not referring to works which could be regarded as divine and miraculous, but ordinary, simple human things—things which would be evidence to God that you are totally surrendered to Him.

Oswald Chambers

A Moment to Refresh

Unwrap the hidden beauties in an ordinary day.

Gerhard E. Frost

❦

The best things are nearest; breath in your nostrils, light in your eyes, flowers at your feet, duties at your hand, the path of God just before you.

Robert Louis Stevenson

God has made everything beautiful for its own time. He has planted eternity in the human heart, but even so, people cannot see the whole scope of God's work from beginning to end.

Ecclesiastes 3:11 NLT

❦

*How beautiful upon the mountains
Are the feet of him Who brings good news,
Who proclaims peace,
Who brings glad tidings of good things,
Who proclaims salvation,
Who says to Zion, "Your God reigns!"*

Isaiah 52:7 NKJV

❦

*The LORD has done many wonderful things! . . .
Everything the LORD does is glorious
and majestic.*

Psalm 111:2–3 CEV

❦

*Our Sovereign, how majestic is your name in
all the earth! You have set your
glory above the heavens.*

Psalm 8:1 NRSV

REMEMBERING WHY

A Moment to Rest

Science fiction is filled with tales of time machines. But in the real world, the only device that can enable you to travel back in time is your memory.

With the aid of photographs, you're ready for your journey to begin. Find one of your old photo albums or open the pictures file on your computer. Choose one you haven't looked at in a while. As you open it up, clear any distractions from your mind. Then sit down, relax, and prepare for a ride back in time.

Take a moment to study each image. Don't skim the photographs. Relive them. Remember why each picture was taken. What made these moments special? Let each one—the people you've known and loved, all the places you've visited, the things you've enjoyed—inspire you to thank God for one positive memory related to each subject or occasion. Thank God that he was with you then and is with you now.

> *A family's photograph album is generally about the extended family and, often, is all that remains of it.*
>
> Susan Sontag

As you close the file or album, take a moment to bring yourself back to the present. Ask yourself, *If I were to give God a photo of me right now, something I wanted him to treasure, where would I want to be and what would I want to be doing?*

A Moment to Reflect

Good people will be remembered as a blessing.

Proverbs 10:7 NCV

Photographs are memories you can hold in your hand.
Eudora Welty said, "A good snapshot stops a moment
from running away." To save that special moment, you
don't have to have a fancy digital camera to get a good
photograph for your memory book.

You can take a mental snapshot. God's gift of memory
automatically creates your own personal scrapbook.
And just like taking a good photo, the secret to captur-
ing picture-perfect memories depends on focus. The
proper way to focus every memory is to view life from
God's perspective. Keeping God's purposes and presence
in mind when you're looking at the past brings clarity
and insight. Memories like this help you learn to use the
past to gain a clearer focus on God's hand in the present.

Hold that pose and smile for me . . .
Let's embrace this priceless memory.
Then, for longer than time will allow,
We can celebrate this gift of "now."

Cathryn Atkinson

❧

Take a good look, friends, at who you were when you got
called into this life. . . . Everything that we have — right
thinking and right living, a clean slate and a fresh start —
comes from God by way of Jesus Christ.

1 Corinthians 1:26, 30 MSG

A Moment to Refresh

The LORD does not see as mortals see; they look on the outward appearance, but the LORD looks on the heart.

1 Samuel 16:7 NRSV

❧

Remember the days of old; consider the generations long past.

Deuteronomy 32:7 NIV

❧

I will cause your name to be remembered in all generations; therefore nations will praise you forever and ever.

Psalm 45:17 ESV

❧

Timothy has come back from his visit with you and has told us about your faith and love. He also said that you always have happy memories of us and that you want to see us as much as we want to see you.

1 Thessalonians 3:6 CEV

❧

We all, with unveiled faces, are reflecting the glory of the Lord and are being transformed into the same image from glory to glory; this is from the Lord who is the Spirit.

2 Corinthians 3:18 HCSB

Treat your friends as you do your pictures, and place them in the best light.

Jennie Jerome Churchill

❧

The value of anything is what the next day's memory of it shall be.

Author Unknown

It's a Wonderful Life

A Moment to Rest

Find time this week to watch the movie *It's a Wonderful Life*, but before hitting Play, reflect on this. Philip Van Doren Stern wrote a story originally called *The Greatest Gift* and sent copies as his Christmas card in 1945. One of them found its way to Frank Capra. The story takes place in a small town, where an average man feels success passed him by. When disaster strikes, he wishes he'd never been born. While not a praying man, George Bailey begs God to show him the way. A guardian angel arrives and shows George that everything valuable in life is right before him.

> *Let no one say we are worthless. God is not a foolish speculator; he would never invest in worthless property.*
>
> Erwin W. Lutzer

Acclaimed by critics and the public, the movie was soon forgotten, until it later became a beloved family classic. Why? *It's a Wonderful Life* mirrors our own doubts, our loss of faith, and the mistaken wish, *If only I were somebody else.* As George wrestles with it all, his wife, Mary, is gentle and supportive, but when things get desperate, she takes control and brings about the miracle they need.

Life doesn't always provide perfect happy endings, but we need this movie's message. Accept who you are, what you have been given, and share it with others.

A Moment to Reflect

*What happens when we live God's way? He brings gifts
into our lives . . . things like affection for others, exuber-
ance about life, serenity. We develop . . .
a sense of compassion in the heart.*

Galatians 5:22 MSG

Have you ever slipped into a George Bailey moment—
pulled from side to side, disheartened, resentful? No
matter how you toil, things happen to push your
dreams out of reach? That's the time to savor a
Clarence-the-Angel moment. Clarence represents the
voice of God, who listens to us and then reminds us
what's important—faith, friends, and family.

As you reflect on your life, realize God is always near,
always approachable, always eager for you to know
how irreplaceable you are. Your life has touched many
others. You have a unique story written just for you.

*Feeling pushed and perplexed,
I want to escape—to find myself.
God knows my soul and I can tell him all.
So I take a fresh path to travel with my Lord, and find
myself on a holy highway full of wonder
and newness and hope.*

Charlotte Adelsperger

❦

*This is what the LORD says: "Stand at the crossroads and
look; ask for the ancient paths, ask where the good way is,
and walk in it, and you will find rest for your souls."*

Jeremiah 6:16 NIV

A Moment to Refresh

The LORD is righteous in everything he does;
he is filled with kindness. The LORD is
close to all who call on him, yes, to all
who call on him sincerely.

Psalm 145:17–18 NLT

❦

God rarely allows
a soul to see
how great a
blessing he is.

Oswald Chambers

I know the best thing we can do
is to always enjoy life.
Ecclesiastes 3:12 CEV

❦

You are the light of the world.
A city that is set on a hill cannot be hidden.
Nor do they light a lamp and put it under a
basket, but on a lampstand, and it gives light
to all who are in the house.
Let your light so shine before men, that they
may see your good works and glorify
your Father in heaven.
Matthew 5:14–16 NKJV

Every life is a
fairy tale, written
by God's fingers.

Hans Christian
Andersen

❦

If you are wise and understand God's ways,
live a life of steady goodness so that
only good deeds will pour forth.
James 3:13 NLT

FREE AS A BIRD

A Moment to Rest

The Bible says that God takes care of the birds of the air. Take a moment to gaze out the window over your kitchen sink or in your office, wherever you have a good view of birds flying.

Watch as they seem to glide effortlessly on the soft air currents and hop joyfully on the ground. If you can go outside, listen to their happy chirping. Notice how they appear to rest free of all care in tree branches, on the roofs of houses, and on telephone lines. Feast your eyes on their marvelous shapes and colors. Imagine how it must feel to be one of them, completely committed to God's care and trusting him to meet your every need.

*No ladder needs
the bird but skies
to situate its
wings,
nor any leader's
grim baton
arraigns it
as it sings.*

Emily Dickinson

Jesus said to observe the birds of the air and see how God takes care of them (Matthew 6). Then he said that you are of much greater value to God than the birds, and wouldn't he watch over you and provide for your needs just as faithfully as he does theirs?

Reflect on that truth for a moment. Then let your imagination take flight. Picture yourself as free as a bird, secure in the care of your heavenly Father.

A Moment to Reflect

Those who wait on the LORD
Shall renew their strength;
They shall mount up with wings like eagles,
They shall run and not be weary,
They shall walk and not faint.

Isaiah 40:31 NKJV

Are you someone who finds it difficult to trust in God for your needs because you believe he expects you to take care of things for yourself? God expects the birds to seek out the food he has scattered about for them and to fly south to avoid the cold winter. He also expects you to do your part, behave responsibly, and obey his commandments.

Still, there are probably some things in your life that you can't manage on your own. For those things, he asks that you trust in him. Trust him to supply your needs, and do not be afraid to ask him to help you. When you do, you will find you are once again able to fly.

All things bright and beautiful,
all creatures great and small,
all things wise and wonderful,
the Lord God made them all.
Each little flower that opens,
each little bird that sings,
he made their glowing colors,
he made their tiny wings.

Cecil Frances Alexander

[The LORD] shielded [Jacob], cared for him, guarded him as the apple of his eye. As an eagle stirs up its nest, and hovers over its young; as it spreads its wings, takes them up, and bears them aloft on its pinions, the LORD alone guided him.

Deuteronomy 32:10–12 NRSV

❧

God said, "Let the water teem with living creatures, and let birds fly above the earth across the expanse of the sky."

Genesis 1:20 NIV

❧

Look at the birds of the air: they neither sow nor reap nor gather into barns, and yet your heavenly Father feeds them. Are you not of more value than they?

Matthew 6:26 ESV

❧

Those who trust in the LORD will find new strength. They will soar high on wings like eagles.

Isaiah 40:31 NLT

❧

Beside them the birds of the heavens dwell; They lift up their voices among the branches.

Psalm 104:12 NASB

The little singing birds sang of God, the animals acclaimed him, the elements feared and the mountains resounded with him, the rivers and springs threw glances toward him, the grasses and flowers smiled.

John Calvin

❧

My soul was always so full of aspirations, that a God was a necessity to me. I was like a bird with an instinct of migration upon me, and a country to migrate to was as essential as it is to the bird.

Hannah Whitall Smith

Breathing Deep

A Moment to Rest

Let go and let God. How many times have you heard that? It sounds like a simple solution, but how does one achieve it? Do you find yourself instead battling to get upstream, struggling against the current, pushing yourself onward? Do you get a few bumps and bruises in the process?

> *The LORD will fulfill his purpose for me; your love, O LORD, endures forever—do not abandon the work of your hands.*
>
> Psalm 138:8 NIV

Contentment requires flexibility, a willingness to bend. Are you resisting something right now? Stand up, take a deep breath, hold it for a few seconds, and then exhale slowly. Bend at the waist and let your arms hang loose. Part company with your tension. Feel it float away.

Remind yourself often that it's easier to bend than to break. There are some things you simply can't control. You may feel like you're at the wheel of a ship, but the rudder is broken and you can't steer. You may have no choice but to sit back and let go. God knows the situation; he knows exactly where you are and where you need to be. Be willing to take that deep breath. Trust God. Because you're flexible, you may end up in a better place than where you'd first planned to go.

A Moment to Reflect

God is working in you, giving you the desire
and the power to do what pleases him.

Philippians 2:13 NLT

The more you yield, the more you become a woman who can be molded like clay in the hand of the potter, your God. He cannot work with clay that is dry or rigid, and he longs to fashion and shape you for his glory, and your best.

It's hard to understand everything that happens and why. But try to practice yielding and bending to whatever life brings. Trust that God is at the wheel, and give him the control. The more flexible you are, the more resilient you'll be to the storms life brings. You will find it easier to bounce right back from disappointments. Your heart will be limber, ready, and more prepared to accept what comes. You may bend, but God will not let you break.

I never really look for anything. What God throws my way
comes. I wake up in the morning and whichever
way God turns my feet, I go.

Pearl Bailey

✤

Teach me to do your will, for you are my God; may your
good Spirit lead me on level ground. For your name's
sake, O LORD, preserve my life; in your righteousness,
bring me out of trouble.

Psalm 143:10–11 NIV

A Moment to Refresh

Lead on, O King
eternal: we follow,
not with fears; for
gladness breaks
like morning
where'er thy face
appears.

Ernest Warburton
Shurtleff

❧

God brings men
into deep waters
not to drown
them, but to
cleanse them.

James H. Aughey

Jeremiah said, "So I went down to the potter's
house and saw him working at the potter's
wheel. He was using his hands to make a pot
from clay, but something went wrong with it.
So he used that clay to make another pot
the way he wanted it to be."

Jeremiah 18:3–4 NCV

❧

If you indeed cry out for insight, and raise your
voice for understanding; if you seek it like silver,
and search for it as for hidden treasures — then
you will understand the fear of the LORD and
find the knowledge of God. For the LORD
gives wisdom; from his mouth come
knowledge and understanding.

Proverbs 2:3–6 NRSV

❧

I have shown you the way that makes sense; I
have guided you along the right path. Your
road won't be blocked, and you won't
stumble when you run.

Proverbs 4:11–12 CEV

❧

You are my rock and my fortress;
Therefore for your name's sake,
Lead me and guide me.

Psalm 31:3 NKJV

GET AWAY

A Moment to Rest

Stop what you're doing—at least inside your head—
and take a few minutes right where you are to get away
and enjoy a little time off. Close your eyes and imagine
a sandy beach, waves lapping at your feet, a refreshing
breeze blowing in off the water. Focus on the way the
sand feels between your toes and how the sun warms
your skin.

You can choose where your thoughts
take you on your getaway. You can be
atop a snow-packed ski slope ready
for the final run of the day, riding a
horse in a forest, or on a train travel-
ing through Europe.

Every woman needs to get away now
and then to refuel emotionally. Your
thoughts are powerful and let you go
anywhere you want to go. Your imaginary destination can be as unique as
you are. It could be to a store filled
with rare books, or perhaps you'd
like to go to an artist colony to try your hand at sketch-
ing. You might enjoy taking classes at Le Cordon Bleu
in Paris to learn cooking techniques. Give yourself the
break you need to get away and get through the day.
Refresh yourself.

> *Life lived amidst
> tension and
> busyness needs
> leisure. Leisure
> that recreates
> and renews.
> Leisure should be
> a time to think
> new thoughts,
> not ponder
> old ills.*
>
> C. Neil Strait

A Moment to Reflect

*Be transformed by the renewing of your minds, so that
you may discern what is the will of God.*

Romans 12:2 NRSV

God used his imagination to create this marvelous universe and all that is in it. Being able to think creatively,
direct your thoughts, and make them work for you are
some of the many talents and abilities he gave you
when he created you in his own image.

When you need a lift to meet the day's demands,
maybe it's time for a refreshing change of scenery. Ask
God to accompany you. Stroll along the water's edge
with him. Share your heart with him as you stand
looking out on a fresh snowfall or walk in a tree-filled
park. Take the time to really look at the beauty around
you. It will energize you and be a good use of your
time—for you and those who depend on you.

*To the quiet mind all things are possible. What is the quiet
mind? A quiet mind is one which nothing weighs on, nothing
worries, which, free from ties and from all self-seeking is
wholly merged into the will of God and dead to its own.*

Meister Eckhart

*Take charge! Take heart! Don't be anxious or get discour-
aged. GOD, my God, is with you in this; he won't
walk off and leave you in the lurch.*

1 Chronicles 28:20 MSG

A Moment to Refresh

*Think of Jesus, whom God sent
to be the High Priest of the
faith we profess.*

Hebrews 3:1 GNT

❧

*We are destroying speculations and every lofty
thing raised up against the knowledge of God,
and we are taking every thought captive
to the obedience of Christ.*

2 Corinthians 10:5 NASB

❧

*The LORD says, "My thoughts are not like
your thoughts. Your ways are not like my
ways. Just as the heavens are higher than the
earth, so are my ways higher than your ways
and my thoughts higher than your thoughts."*

Isaiah 55:8–9 NCV

❧

*God cares for you, so turn all
your worries over to him.*

1 Peter 5:7 CEV

❧

*I recall all you have done, O LORD; I remember
your wonderful deeds of long ago. They are
constantly in my thoughts.*

Psalm 77:11–12 NLT

*Our life is what
our thoughts
make it.*

Catherine of Siena

❧

*My thoughts are
my company; I
can bring them
together, select
them, detain them,
dismiss them.*

Walter Savage
Landor

GOD'S PLAN

A Moment to Rest

Sit back in your favorite chair and reflect on the events of your day. Did you receive a comforting hug, a word of encouragement, or a new insight that you hadn't expected? These are no chance encounters, only God-arranged pieces of his master plan for you. Ordinary encounters that appear as coincidences are really God's loving hand on your life.

> *"I know the plans I have for you," declares the LORD, "plans to prosper you and not to harm you, plans to give you hope and a future."*
>
> Jeremiah 29:11
> NIV

We don't usually see God's overall plan. Wouldn't it be great if our story was part of a feature film and the plot line was mapped out in detail for us? We'd have specific directives for what to do, and we could avoid painful detours. Life, however, is more like a series of short vignettes, the purposes of which may be hidden for the moment.

In time, your life will be revealed and understood. You will be able to look back and see how your experiences fit together like a perfectly crafted puzzle. But for now, God wants only your willingness to agree to his plan in the slow and mysterious ways he sets it in motion. Whenever you feel anxious, just review God's promises and tuck them in your heart. God's plans for you are good.

A Moment to Reflect

We have continued praying for you, asking God that you will know fully what he wants. We pray that you will also have great wisdom and understanding in spiritual things so that you will live the kind of life that honors and pleases the Lord in every way.

Colossians 1:9–10 NCV

When you remind yourself every day that nothing is by chance with God, it calms the heart. Trusting that he is completely in charge of every detail can give you relief from burdens you need not carry.

Look at every situation, even the difficult ones, as an instrument for God to use for your ultimate good. Don't miss seeing God encourage you through faithful, praying friends or teach you through a stranger. Say in your heart, "That's you, God, isn't it?" You will be astounded at the innumerable ways in which you see him craft his master plan.

When you're cast about by the storms of life,
When your days are filled with doubt or strife,
When nothing makes sense, it's hard to stand,
Remember this—God has a plan.
God has a plan, keep clinging to this,
Forget your agenda, look to his.
As you walk by faith, cling to his hand,
Remember this, God has a plan.

Jan McIntosh

A Moment to Refresh

Perhaps you've been pondering your future plans and feel perplexed. Just remember Moses, who went from the pond, to the palace, to the pasture, to the pinnacle, to view the Promised Land before entering paradise. Praise the Lord!

Patsy Clairmont

❦

When we are rightly related to God, life is full of spontaneous joyful uncertainty and expectancy. We do not know what God is going to do next; he packs our life with surprises.

Oswald Chambers

God has also given riches and wealth to every man, and He has allowed him to enjoy them, take his reward, and rejoice in his labor. This is a gift of God, for he does not often consider the days of his life because God keeps him occupied with the joy of his heart.

Ecclesiastes 5:19–20 HCSB

❦

"I make known the end from the beginning, from ancient times what is still to come. I say: My purpose will stand, and I will do all that I please."

Isaiah 46:10 NIV

❦

To everything there is a season, A time for every purpose under heaven.

Ecclesiastes 3:1 NKJV

❦

He who began a good work in you will perfect it until the day of Christ Jesus.

Philippians 1:6 NASB

❦

We know that for those who love God all things work together for good, for those who are called according to his purpose.

Romans 8:28 ESV

GOLD MEDAL PERFORMANCE

A Moment to Rest

The Olympic Games take place every four years, but you can mount the winner's platform right now. Cheering fans fill the stadium. A trumpet fanfare sounds in the air. A massive torch burns brightly nearby. And there you are on the highest platform, awaiting the gold.

Think back over your life and consider if you deserve a gold medal for any of the roles you've played: friend, mother, wife, employee, child of God. Have your efforts exceeded your own expectations? Have you kept going, even when the odds were not in your favor? What accomplishments have given you the greatest pleasure? Have you given your all?

> *The applause of a single human being is of great importance.*
>
> Samuel Johnson

Picture a gold medal being placed around your neck for each of these victories. Listen to the national anthem playing in your honor. Celebrate the satisfaction of a job well done.

When it comes to daily life, you have this same opportunity, with or without the fanfare. One significant difference is that though it may feel like you're in competition with the rest of the world, in reality God has placed you in a solo event. No one can achieve the gold medal for your life except you.

A Moment to Reflect

God is not unjust. He will not forget how hard you have worked for him and how you have shown your love to him by caring for other believers.

Hebrews 6:10 NLT

Praise, accolades, and applause are great motivators. So is applause from those around you. Even more important, however, is the applause of the One who made you. The moments in your life that make God proud may look very different from the ones that come to your mind and seem medal worthy, but they are a bigger cause of celebration.

When you achieve something noteworthy in your life, whether publicly or privately, make a point of inviting God to the victory party. Every one of your accomplishments is a joint effort—God supplies you with the talents and opportunities to win, and your job is to go for the gold with passion and perseverance.

I do not ask for any crown
But that which all may win;
Nor try to conquer any world
Except the one within.
Be thou my guide until I find,
Led by a tender hand,
The happy kingdom in myself
And dare to take command.

Louisa May Alcott

Each of you has been blessed with one of God's many wonderful gifts to be used in the service of others. So use your gift well.

1 Peter 4:10 CEV

Charm can fool you, and beauty can trick you, but a woman who respects the LORD should be praised. Give her the reward she has earned; she should be praised in public for what she has done.

Proverbs 31:30–31 NCV

Each one's work will become obvious, for the day will disclose it, because it will be revealed by fire; the fire will test the quality of each one's work.

1 Corinthians 3:13 HCSB

Having then gifts differing according to the grace that is given to us, let us use them.

Romans 12:6 NKJV

Whatever you do, do your work heartily, as for the Lord rather than for men.

Colossians 3:23 NASB

Applause is the spur of noble minds, the end and aim of weak ones.

Charles Caleb Colton

Let us work as if success depended on ourselves alone, but with the heartfelt conviction that we are doing nothing and God everything.

Ignatius of Loyola

AIMING FOR EXCELLENCE

A Moment to Rest

Take a quiet walk through your neighborhood or a nearby park. Let the gentle wind and rustle of the leaves quiet your heart. Then ponder this: "Do I strive for perfection in my life?" Perhaps you don't strive for perfection all the time, but are there some areas of your life where you feel that you just don't measure up to what you "should" be? Do you keep trying to be a better woman, but your efforts never seem to be good enough? Does it seem that somebody keeps raising the mark on the measuring stick a few notches higher? (Now, who could that be?)

> *What is Christian perfection? Loving God with all our heart, mind, soul, and strength.*
>
> John Wesley

Striving for perfection is an impossible quest; perfection is a myth and forever out of reach. Aim for excellence, instead. Excellence has nothing to do with outward appearances or with what you accomplish or with what you possess. Excellence depends solely on what you are from God's perspective—and God does not focus on your flaws.

When you seek God's ideal, you will throw away your measuring stick. You don't need one that marks success and quality of life by the world's standards. Jesus requires only simplicity of heart.

A Moment to Reflect

Blessed are you, O LORD; teach me your statutes.

Psalm 119:12 NRSV

God judges a woman by her character, by her pursuits in life. As you consider this, ask God to bring out all that is excellent in you. Let him shape you with faithfulness, honor, and integrity. Be aware of how he adds these finishing touches in a way that will give glory to him and satisfaction and meaning for you.

Be ready to radiate from the inside out. Outward change will be perceptible but subtle—a sparkle in the eye, a tilt of the head, a lilt to the walk—but you'll know the inward change makes the difference.

If you check out the life of Jesus you will discover what made him perfect. He did not attain a state of perfection by carrying around in his pocket a list of rules and regulations, or by seeking to conform to the cultural mores of the time. He was perfect because he never made a move without his Father.

Tom Skinner

❦

Keep your eyes on Jesus, who both began and finished this race we're in. Study how he did it. Because he never lost sight of where he was headed—that exhilarating finish in and with God—he could put up with anything along the way: cross, shame, whatever. And now he's there, in the place of honor, right alongside God.

Hebrews 12:2 MSG

A Moment to Refresh

There is nothing you can do to make God love you more. There is nothing you can do to make God love you less. His love is unconditional, impartial, everlasting, infinite, perfect. God is love!

Author Unknown

❧

Of all classes and descriptions of persons on this earth, they are the happiest of whom it may be said that the things most hoped for by them are the things not seen.

Mennonite
Writings

You were taught to be made new in your hearts, to become a new person. That new person is made to be like God—made to be truly good and holy.

Ephesians 4:23–24 NCV

❧

Show me your ways, O LORD, teach me your paths; guide me in your truth and teach me, for you are God my Savior, and my hope is in you all day long.

Psalm 25:4–5 NIV

❧

God is my strong refuge; He makes my way perfect.

2 Samuel 22:33 HCSB

❧

People judge by outward appearance, but the LORD looks at the heart.

1 Samuel 16:7 NLT

❧

I run toward the goal, so that I can win the prize of being called to heaven.

Philippians 3:14 CEV

TIME TO LET IT GO

A Moment to Rest

Carrying around anger and resentment weighs more heavily on your mind and heart than five pounds of cellulite does on your thighs. It's time to give your heart a break. Sit down and write a letter to someone you need to forgive. Write out all your angry thoughts and feelings, every offense and slight. Tell that person exactly how you feel. Don't leave out a thing.

When you've got it all down on paper, place your hands on the paper and open your heart. Ask God to help you cross over to forgiveness. Then, to demonstrate your intentions, write a final paragraph to your letter. Note that you are choosing to forgive and that God is helping you

A person's ability to forgive is in proportion to the greatness of his soul.

Author Unknown

to bring your thoughts and emotions in line with that choice. When you're through writing, thank God for helping you. Finish by ripping the letter into small pieces and tossing it in the trash.

Forgiving someone from the heart takes time. You may have to go to God more than once, asking for the strength to let go of deep-seated resentment and to experience true healing. But forgiveness is God's specialty. With his help, it can become yours as well.

A Moment to Reflect

*Be kind to one another, tender-hearted, forgiving each
other, just as God in Christ also has forgiven you.*

Ephesians 4:32 NASB

Don't wait for apologies, reconciliation, or even understanding. Make the first move toward forgiveness.
Holding on to resentment is like gorging on junk food
because someone called you fat. All you end up doing is
hurting yourself. So let it go and lose that heavy feeling
you've been carrying around.

Like losing weight of any kind, forgiving from the heart
is hard work. You may have to write several letters before
you've really worked through your feelings. But it will be
worth it. Once again, you'll be free to laugh, to love, and
to enjoy life. And the lighthearted, invigorating, refreshing feeling in your heart is the first benefit you'll feel as
that weight is lifted off your mind and spirit.

*Endeavor to be always patient of the faults and imperfections
of others; for thou hast many faults and imperfections of
thine own that require forbearance. If thou art not able to
make thyself that which thou wishest, how canst thou expect
to mold another in conformity to thy will?*

Thomas à Kempis

*Jesus said, "If you forgive men when they sin against you,
your heavenly Father will also forgive you."*

Matthew 6:14 NIV

Just as the Lord has forgiven you, so also you must forgive.

Colossians 3:13 HCSB

❦

Peter came to Him and said, "Lord, how often shall my brother sin against me, and I forgive him? Up to seven times?" Jesus said to him, "I do not say to you, up to seven times, but up to seventy times seven."

Matthew 18:21–22 NKJV

❦

Jesus prayed, "Forgive us our sins, just as we have forgiven those who have sinned against us."

Matthew 6:12 NLT

❦

Jesus said, "When you are praying, if you are angry with someone, forgive him so that your Father in heaven will also forgive your sins."

Mark 11:25 NCV

❦

Jesus said, "Don't judge others, and God won't judge you. Don't be hard on others, and God won't be hard on you. Forgive others, and God will forgive you."

Luke 6:37 CEV

Humanity is never so beautiful as when praying for forgiveness, or else forgiving another.

Jean Paul Richter

❦

The only true for- giveness is that which is offered and extended even before the offender has apologized and sought it.

Søren Kierkegaard

TAKE A CHANCE

A Moment to Rest

Do you have dreams for the future, prospects you'd like to explore in your life? A new career, a home business, a challenging hobby? Is it hard for you to take steps into the unknown? Does an old fear knock on the door and tell you to forget it, you can't do it, it is out of your reach?

God has not given us a spirit of timidity, but of power and love and discipline.

2 Timothy 1:7
NASB

Picture in your mind a pioneer woman starting out on a great adventure by going across the plains to settle a new land in the West. Imagine the courage it took to leave the comfort and security behind to venture forth, to be a part of settling a new and untamed land. She probably had a healthy dose of fear, too, but it didn't keep her from taking a chance.

Is there a pioneer inside of you? Talk to God today about pursuing your dreams. Ask him to go forward ⸱ʰ you, to be at your side as you explore new regions ᵗlife. Listen for his answers. Trust him to give ɑnd enthusiasm, to share the risks with ᵧ which roads to take, which cor- ᵣself, I can do it with God's

HEART

*Such is the confidence that we have through Christ toward
God. Not that we are competent of ourselves
to claim anything as coming from us; our
competence is from God.*

2 Corinthians 3:4–5 NRSV

Confidence in God is essential for the pioneer. With faith comes the boldness you need. When you pursue the dreams God has placed in your heart and use the gifts and talents he's given you, there is no reason to fear. No dream is too big for him.

There will be setbacks and disappointments, but as someone said, the one who tries something and fails is much better off than the one who tries to do nothing and succeeds. Look ahead with hope and anticipation as you step out beyond your limitations. Your faith and a willingness to take chances will make your dreams a reality.

*Deep in every woman lies a vast frontier,
Horizons to explore, dream-wagons to steer.
As in the past, those days of old,
The way is dusty and sometimes cold.
When clouds of doubt should appear
Know you are made for faith, not fear.
You must find your way, be bold enough to dare,
With provision from the Lord and security in prayer.*

Jan Coleman

A Moment to Refresh

We are all faced
with a series of
great opportunities
brilliantly dis-
guised as impossi-
ble situations.

Charles Swindoll

Mountain-moving
faith is not just
dreaming and
desiring. It is dar-
ing to risk failure.

Mary Kay Ash

*May He grant you according
to your heart's desire,
And fulfill all your purpose.*

Psalm 20:4 NKJV

*Take delight in the LORD, and he will
give you your heart's desires.*

Psalm 37:4 NLT

*Don't be afraid. I am with you. Don't tremble
with fear. I am your God.
I will make you strong.*

Isaiah 41:10 CEV

*The moment I called out, you stepped in; you
made my life large with strength.*

Psalm 138:3 MSG

*May the God of hope fill you with all joy and
peace as you trust in him, so that you may
overflow with hope by the power
of the Holy Spirit.*

Romans 15:13 NIV

*Many plans are in a man's mind, but it is the
Lord's purpose for him that will stand.*

Proverbs 19:21 AMP

DAILY JOY

A Moment to Rest

Kids know how to find happiness in simple, unexpected places. An empty box, a big pile of leaves, a puddle of mud . . . Want to feel like a kid again? Blow bubbles. Fill a small saucer with dishwashing liquid and fashion a paper clip into a loop. Dip the paper clip into the solution, then lift and blow.

See how far you can blow the bubbles across the room. Watch how quickly they pop. Note their color and size. Try to outdo yourself for the biggest bubble or the most bubbles created in one blow.

There is not one blade of grass, there is no color in the world that is not intended to make us rejoice.

John Calvin

Now, dip a little deeper into your heart. Sure, it's fun to blow bubbles. But happiness is as fleeting as the bubbles you're blowing. Joy, however, is something that is infinitely sturdier than a fragile film of soap floating in the air. It's something that bubbles up from deep inside regardless of season or circumstance.

As you blow bubbles, reflect on times of true joy in your life, such as a visitor who appeared when you needed them, a loved one's recovery from an illness, or a surprising answer to prayer. Ask God to show you how to nurture a deeper joy in your daily life.

A Moment to Reflect

This is the day that the LORD has made;
let us rejoice and be glad in it.

Psalm 118:24 ESV

One universal act that will help fill your life with daily joy is to know God. The better you get to know him through reading the Bible, praying, doing what you believe he is leading you to do, and seeing him work in the lives of your friends and family, the more joy you'll discover you have and be able to share.

Joy is the result—the reward—of becoming reconnected to the one who created you, the One who loves you and gave his life for you. In his presence you will find your heart bubbling over with joy.

As the hand is made for holding and the eye for seeing, you
have fashioned me, O Lord, for joy. Share with me the vision
to find joy everywhere: in the wild violet's beauty, in the lark's
melody, in the face of a steadfast man, in a child's smile, in a
mother's love, in the purity of Jesus.

Scottish Celtic Prayer

❧

The LORD is my strength and shield. I trust him with all my
heart. He helps me, and my heart is filled with joy.
I burst out in songs of thanksgiving.

Psalm 28:7 NLT

*The signposts of GOD are clear and point out
the right road. The life-maps of GOD are right,
showing the way to joy.*

Psalm 19:7–8 MSG

❦

*You will show me the path of life;
In Your presence is fullness of joy;
At Your right hand are pleasures forevermore.*

Psalm 16:11 NKJV

❦

Shout joyfully to God, all the earth!

Psalm 66:1 HCSB

❦

*Sing to Him a new song;
Play skillfully
with a shout of joy.*

Psalm 33:3 NASB

❦

*My brothers and sisters, when you have many
kinds of troubles, you should be full of joy,
because you know that these troubles test your
faith, and this will give you patience.*

James 1:2–3 NCV

*Joy is the surest
sign of the
presence
of God.*

Pierre Teilhard de
Chardin

❦

*We are all strings
in the concert of
his joy; the spirit
from his mouth
strikes the note
and the tune of
our strings.*

Jakob Böehme

LOVE COMES BACK

A Moment to Rest

Think of a boomerang, and what comes to mind? A bent or curved stick that you throw high in the air. It swings around and comes right back to the thrower's hand. One of the most remarkable tools in history was invented by the Australian Aborigines. It was actually the first man-made flying machine, an amazing hunk of wood that works on complex principles of physics. If you want it to come back to you, there are certain techniques that must be mastered.

> *Love is like the five loaves and two fishes. It doesn't start to multiply until you give it away.*
>
> Author Unknown

You are familiar with the saying "Love isn't love until you give it away." Like the boomerang, love is an action, an activity. Love is not just something we feel; rather, love is something we do. It's easy to master. Just throw love away, high and wide. Give love as much and as often as you can. You'll be surprised how much comes right back to you.

Consider ways you can give away love this week. Take a meal to someone who's ill. Write a note of encouragement and include a little cash for someone in need. Baby-sit for a single mom. Give love freely and watch it return to you from unexpected places.

A Moment to Reflect

Everything the Lord does is right.
He is loyal to all he has made.

Psalm 145:17 NCV

When one loves God, it is natural to pass on that love to others, for love is the fundamental nature of God. When one is filled to the brim with the affirming love of the heavenly Father, love springs forth. When you cast forth love to others, you embody the commandment to love one another as Christ loved you.

As you give yourself with joy to others, others will see God in you, and his love will come back to you. It may be as warm thanks from a special friend or a smile from a stranger, but however it comes back, you'll be lifted higher than you can imagine.

You can smell it in a flower,
You can see it in the sky,
You can feel it soft and gentle
As a summer breeze blows by —
The touch of love is in the air!
You can show it with a smile,
You will know it when you pray,
It's a gift that's all around you
And inside you every day —
God's touch of love is everywhere!

Alice Joyce Davidson

A Moment to Refresh

A new commandment I give to you, that you love one another; as I have loved you, that you also love one another. By this all will know that you are My disciples.

John 13:34–35 NKJV

❧

May mercy, peace, and love be multiplied to you.

Jude 1:2 HCSB

❧

Love never ends.

1 Corinthians 13:8 NCV

❧

We love because he first loved us. . . . Whoever loves God must also love his brother.

1 John 4:19, 21 ESV

❧

Be imitators of God, therefore, as dearly loved children and live a life of love, just as Christ loved us and gave himself up for us as a fragrant offering and sacrifice to God.

Ephesians 5:1–2 NIV

❧

Jesus knew that the time had come to leave this world. . . . Having loved his dear companions, he continued to love them right to the end.

John 13:1 MSG

Love is the only force capable of transforming an enemy into a friend.

Martin Luther King Jr.

❧

Love cures people—both the ones who give it and the ones who receive it.

Karl Augustus Menninger

QUIET WITHIN

A Moment to Rest

Clutter, clamor, and distractions are as much a part of a woman's life as breathing. Appointments, deadlines, meetings, family responsibilities, emergency trips to the grocery or drugstore, clothes to be washed. But there's a quiet spot waiting to be found inside you this very minute—a tiny, tranquil glimpse of heaven you can visit even if your feet are currently planted in a mountain of dirty laundry.

Getting there begins with dropping your worries, like laundry into a hamper, at God's feet. Big or small, legitimate or obsessive, every concern of yours is a concern of his. Close your eyes and take several deep breaths and shrug several times to release any tension in your neck and shoulders. Then, picture yourself sitting quietly in God's presence. This is no illusion. He's there.

Next, take an unencumbered mental stroll through the streets of heaven with Jesus by your side. While your mind isn't capable of knowing what that would really be like, you can be sure it will be an experience filled with absolute peace— the peace only God can give. Bask in it. Enjoy a taste, if just for a moment, of what it means to be truly at rest.

> *What peace and inward quiet should he have who would cut away from himself all busyness of mind, and think only on heavenly things.*
>
> Thomas à Kempis

A Moment to Reflect

*Our citizenship is in heaven, and from it we
await a Savior, the Lord Jesus Christ.*

Philippians 3:20 ESV

Finding and experiencing peace in a chaotic world isn't
natural—it's supernatural. God's peace bears little
resemblance to what the world promises will soothe
your worried heart and mind. That's because God's
peace doesn't depend on favorable circumstances. It pre-
vails no matter what's going on in the world around you
with your family, your job, your friends, or your heart.

You can bring much-needed relief to your worried mind
by understanding that God is always with you, waiting
to apply his peace to each situation. And the peace he
makes available to you here on earth is but a foretaste of
what you will experience one day in heaven. You can
depend on it.

*Drop thy still dews of quietness,
Till all our strivings cease;
Take from our souls the strain and stress,
And let our ordered lives confess
The beauty of thy peace.*

John Greenleaf Whittier

A Moment to Refresh

A heart at peace gives life to the body.

Proverbs 14:30 NIV

❧

You will keep him in perfect peace,
Whose mind is stayed on You,
Because he trusts in You.

Isaiah 26:3 NKJV

❧

May the Lord of peace Himself continually
grant you peace in every circumstance.

2 Thessalonians 3:16 NASB

❧

The LORD gives his people strength; the
LORD blesses his people with peace.

Psalm 29:11 HCSB

❧

Let the peace of Christ rule in your hearts, to
which indeed you were called in one body.
And be thankful.

Colossians 3:15 ESV

❧

God has something stored up for you in
heaven, where it will never decay or be
ruined or disappear.

1 Peter 1:4 CEV

The time of business does not differ from the time of prayer; and in the noise and clutter of my kitchen, while several persons are at the same time calling for different things, I possess God in as great a tranquility as if I were upon my knees at the Blessed Sacrament.

Brother Lawrence

❧

O God, make us children of quietness and heirs of peace.

Clement of Rome

Never be in a hurry; do everything quietly and in a calm spirit. Do not lose your inner peace for anything whatsoever, even if your whole world seems upset.

Francis de Sales